The *Saga* of a Chanting Phoenix

Alice Chudes

PARTRIDGE

Copyright © 2020 by Alice Chudes.

Library of Congress Control Number: 2020911462
ISBN: Hardcover 978-1-5437-5898-6
Softcover 978-1-5437-5896-2
eBook 978-1-5437-5897-9

All rights reserved. No part of this book may be used or reproduced by any means, graphic, electronic, or mechanical, including photocopying, recording, taping or by any information storage retrieval system without the written permission of the author except in the case of brief quotations embodied in critical articles and reviews.

Because of the dynamic nature of the Internet, any web addresses or links contained in this book may have changed since publication and may no longer be valid. The views expressed in this work are solely those of the author and do not necessarily reflect the views of the publisher, and the publisher hereby disclaims any responsibility for them.

For more information about the book, please visit www.alicechudes.com and www.store-alicechudes.com.
Illustrated by Ellie Lasthiotaki, www.ellielasthiotaki.com.
With a foreword by Vladimir Guevarra.

Print information available on the last page.

To order additional copies of this book, contact
Toll Free +65 3165 7531 (Singapore)
Toll Free +60 3 3099 4412 (Malaysia)
orders.singapore@partridgepublishing.com

www.partridgepublishing.com/singapore

Dedicated to my grandfather Alexander

Contents

Acknowledgements xiii
It Is Hard Dealing with a Poet by Vladimir Guevarra xv
Foreword by Vladimir Guevarra: Reading Alice Chudes' Romantic
and Relatable Verses xix
Preface: My Poetry Interpretation xxiii

DEFINING TIMELESSNESS

Wisdom Is an All-Encompassing Heavenly Ode 4
Truth Is What You Hear When You Stand Still 8
Time Is Spiral Like DNA 12
Soul Is an Intangible Quintessence of Life 14
Knowledge Germinates the Enlightenment Seed 18
Light in a Kaleidoscope Heals in Time of Self-Doubt 22
Love Grows the Wings to Touch Infinity 26
Life Is a Rose with Thorns 30
Happiness Is to Be in Tune with the World 32
Dreams Are Answers from the Subconscious 34
Destiny Is Carving Out My Path in Poetry 38
Abundance Is Being Wealthy with What Is Within One's Grasp 42

PHOENIX'S SAGA IN CHANTED POETRY

2015–2020 Resurrecting Through the Tears of Love 46

I Saw You in One Wicked and Forbidden Dream 48
Metamorphosis: Painting the Mandala of My Past to Release My
New Future 54

Truth Is, You Never Left Me	58
A Fortune Stroke of Serendipity	62
Ink's Power to Heal	64
My Unicorn at the Genesis of the New World	66
The Eye of the Perfect Storm	70
Revelations in Turbulent Times	74
Catching My Muse, My Firebird	78
A Blessing in Disguise	80
Sacrificial Lambs	82
A Seed of Knowledge	86
A Leap of Faith	90
My Anointed Future	94
A Cry of My Soul	98
#MeToo	100
It Is Time to Act	102
The World on Fire	104
Six Senses in Jerusalem	106
Thanksgiving to God	112
A Glimpse at Apocalypse	114
A Message in a Bottle	118
Lost Without Hope	122
My Outside-the-Box Mantra	126
Truth Always Leaks Out	132
A Sight of the Parallel World	134
A Hymn for My Subconscious Mind	136
I Wish I Were Not Alone	138
A Million Shattered Pieces	140
Walking in Your Footsteps	142
The Secret Love Potion	146
I Wander. I Wonder. I Speak to the Stars	150
A Weeping Soul in the River of Life	154
An Illusion of Separation	158
Two Acquainted Strangers	162
A Medium in Love	164
A Night Silver Lining	166
Subject to Interpretation	172
You Are My Cup of Tea!	174
Oh, Baby, Hear My Questions!	178

Reunion: It Is Not Too Late! 180
An Unanswered Invitation 184
Adieu to He Who Does Not Exist 186
One Dreadful Step Ahead 190
If I Were Your Queen! 192
Creator's Calling 194
Love Is Way More Durable Than Hatred 196

2005–2015 The Lost Decade 198

1995–2005 Discovering Love, the Essence of Life 202

Deux Colombes, l'Âme de l'Océan 204
Dove's Happiness Scent.. 204
Mon Cœur Rayonne 208
A Beam from My Heart 208
La Fève de la Galette des Rois 210
Twelfth Night Cake's Charm 210
Tu Es Mon Étoile Filante 212
You Are My Shooting Star 212
L'Aspiration d'une Petite Fille 214
The Yearning of a Little Girl 214
A Thought of Gratitude 218
La Soif de Liberté 220
Thirst for Freedom 220
Une Heureuse Pensée à Propos de la Vie 222
A Happy Thought About Life.. 222
La Brume de Demain... 224
The Mist of Destiny.. 224
Le Courant de la Vie 226
The Current of Life.. 226
A Restless Traveller 228
A Motherly Gaze 230
Dancing Snow.. 232
A Rhetorical Question for Motherland 234
Enlevée par le Vent... 238
The Other Side of the Mirror.. 238

Une Lettre d'Amour 242
A Love Letter 242
The Music of My Heart 244
Un Rêve de Midi 248
A Midday Dream 248
Tombée Amoureuse 250
Fallen in Love 250
À l'Amie du Cœur 252
To My Dear Friend 252
Une Lettre à Ma Fille 254
A Letter to My Daughter 254
The Hidden Sense of Life...256
Une Vague Idée de l'Amour 258
A Faint Image of Love..258
La Lumière Divine 260
The Divine Light 260
Will the World Ever Change?.. 262
A Play on Words 264

Afterword: My Musings about Life 266
List of Illustrations: by Alice Chudes.. 270
List of Illustrations: by Ellie Lasthiotaki.. 272

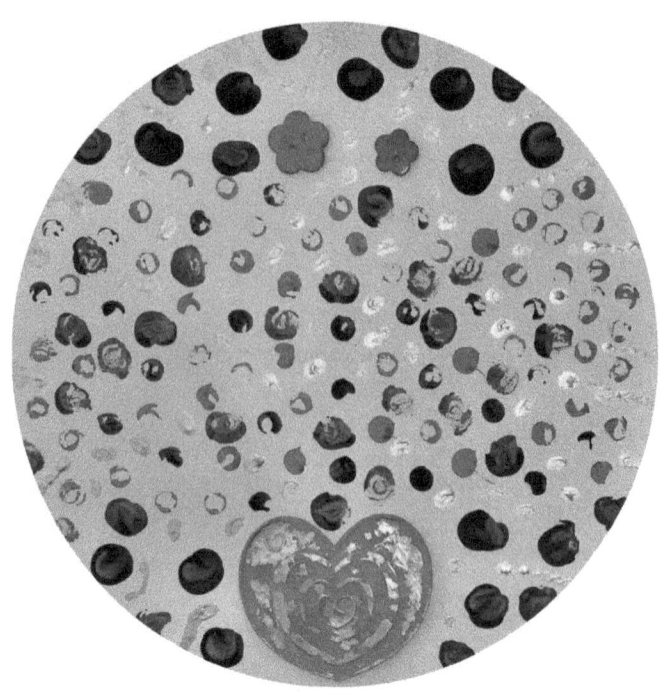

The Pink-Golden Explosion of Love, 2020
Acrylic and mixed media on circular canvas 50 cm
Illustration by Alice Chudes

> Dove 🕊 came in to him at eventide,
> and, lo, in mouth an olive leaf* freshly plucked;
> so, Noah knew that the waters were abated from off the Earth.**
> –Genesis 8:11

---

*   An olive leaf, in Hebrew: עלֵה זית [alay zayit], is a sign of life after the Flood and of God's bringing Noah, his family, and the animals to the firm land.

** The Talmud compares the spirit of God hovering over the waters to a dove that hovers over her young. In the post-biblical Judaism, souls are envisioned as bird-like (Bahir 119), a concept that may be derived from the Biblical notion that dead spirits 'chirp' (Isa. 29:4). The Guf, or the Treasury of Souls, is sometimes described as a columbarium, a dove cote. This connects it to a related legend: the 'Palace of the Bird's Nest', the dwelling place of the Messiah's soul until his or her advent (Zohar II: 8a–9a). The Vilna Gaon explicitly declares that a dove is a symbol of the human soul (Commentary to Jonah, 1). The dove is also a symbol of the People of Israel (Song of Songs Rabbah 2:14), an image frequently repeated in Midrash.

ACKNOWLEDGEMENTS

> If you can cultivate the right attitude,
> your enemies are your best spiritual teachers
> because their presence provides you with the opportunity
> to enhance and develop tolerance, patience, and understanding.
> —Dalai Lama XIV

First, I would like to thank every single one of my friends who have always kept their door *closed** for me. I cannot possibly mention every person who helped me here. However, please know that all your names are forever written in The Book of Life.

Second, I would like to thank every single one of my enemies. Why would anyone thank his or her enemies? – I would like to thank you because each time I met an obstacle in my life, thanks to you, you redirected me from the wrong path to the right one.

Finally, I would like to thank my most favourite category of people, the converters. As per the last chapter of 'The Art of War' by Sun Tzu, these are people who started off by being my enemies but with the passage of time converted to be my friends. They have already come to apologise or will do precisely that in the near future. They do not have to tell me, whether they intend to do so or not. Maybe because it is already written in the history of the world. Remember that time is spiral like DNA. It is not linear. It is the cobra snake that eats its own tail. Everything that is about to happen, happened already. Furthermore, these are my most favourite people, because they are my most loyal supporters. Once they turn around by apologising, there is no way back to hatred. They can only love from that point on.

Любовь спасет мир. - Нет! - *Любовь уже спасла мир. И не раз, и не два!***

However, I won't tell you all the answers …

To be continued.

---

*   *'Closed'*, as opposed to 'open'.
** From Russian, 'Love will save the world. - Incorrect! - *Love has already saved the world.* And not once or twice!'

Self-Portrait, 2016
Acrylic on canvas 45 by 35 cm

It Is Hard Dealing with a Poet

by Vladimir Guevarra

It is hard dealing with a poet
For he looks at the world in a certain way
A certain angle
Misconstrued and mangled
Nothing is in between
And everything is in extremes

It is hard dealing with a poet
For he has an opinion much greater and much better than anybody else's
And all fact is hearsay, and history is myth

It is hard dealing with a poet
For books are like friends, and words keep him company
In days of fluid motion and nights of lunacy

It is hard dealing with a poet
Who writes of tormented souls, tortured love
Quivering flesh, distorted hate, and his perfect self
He curses the blackness of the heart and the brilliance of an evil mind
He understands everything in the world
Yet squanders each silver coin in his pocket

It is hard dealing with a poet
Who searches for answers where there are none
Who studies mankind's place amongst the cosmos and the stars
Who wonders about his Creator and his Destroyer
And who makes the simplest things difficult, and the complex ones absurd

It is hard dealing with a poet
Enamoured by a woman
The scent of her hair, the warmth of her skin
The contours of her body, and her blood hot within

Continued

Continuation

It is hard dealing with a poet
Who stares at paintings and murals over and over like a maniac obsessed
And convinces himself that reality mimics art, and art is perfection
Where sketches trace the contours of society
And society is his moving subject

It is hard dealing with a poet
Who demands accuracy and excellence
When he himself is frail, flawed, and broken
When he can't listen to what people say of him
And confuses people with his verses

It is hard dealing with a poet
Who easily feels 'at peace' looking at hyacinths
In striking hues of blue, yellow, and white
Or in fragrant fields of lavender
Across rolling hills with yonder cliffs and crashing waves

It is hard dealing with a poet
Who loosens his tongue after cavorting with wine
Who lashes sharp dictates against fellow saints
And whispers saccharine lyrics to fellow sinners

Alas, such is the sheltered life of the petit bourgeois punk poet
Who lies on his bed sleepless, worrying over trivial things
And doesn't have the police knocking on his door
He walks in circles, lost in a cycle of lumpen culture and useless drivel
Unfeeling towards poverty and the crisis that spewed it
For he couldn't understand the point of understanding the world

Continued

Continuation

But the best of poets are of a different type
For they are warriors too
With machine guns wrought with ideology
And bullets forged with vengeance
They know their place in history
And see how the few masters exploit the earth and their many slaves

The words they use are deliberate yet chaotic
And meant to crush the fortresses of fascism
They speak of the people, and the people speak of them

Their songs of emancipation are scoffed at by sycophants of the old ways
But are tender lullabies to children born of the new world
Each poem has a purpose
And the best poets know their enemies

Sea Is the Mirror of Ourselves, 2018
Acrylic and oil on canvas 150 by 100 cm

Foreword

by Vladimir Guevarra:

Reading Alice Chudes' Romantic and Relatable Verses

> The aim of art is to represent not the outward appearance of things, but their inward significance.
> —Aristotle

The world has become such a busy place that often many of us forget the art of connecting with fellow humans, pausing awhile, breathing, reading, contemplating, and exhaling.

Alice Chudes is one such person who would frequently pause and contemplate, as is obvious in her poetry. Growing up in Russia, studying and living in countries like the United States, the United Kingdom, and Singapore, working in fields as demanding as the capital markets, investing, and public relations, Alice Chudes could be forgiven if she was caught up altogether in the affairs of the capitalist world. Her soul is intact, and that is the most important. In my previous life as a financial journalist, I have seen executives who have become too sucked up by the markets and by money, to the point of losing their soul.

In this collection of poems, Alice Chudes eschews all those modern trappings, and exposes herself almost in a fragile manner. Her poems reveal her vulnerability and honesty. She shows devotion to family, to her grandfather, her father and mother, as well as to her native Russia. She has an unshaking belief in a supreme Deity, and this belief effuses in Alice Chudes' verses—romantic, sensual, passionate, romanticised, and positive.

Alice Chudes is also a polyglot; it is an altogether great achievement for her to write poems other than in her native Russian. She composes in English as well as in French and then writes literary interpretations in English.

Make no mistake, though. Alice Chudes writes with intent. She draws the reader in, into her psyche, and convinces the reader to help improve the human condition—whether it be with family, society, or the Earth.

It is perhaps timely for Alice Chudes to publish her poetry, with her recurring themes of challenges, of love, of regret—at a time when the world is plagued by a new pandemic, the COVID-19 coronavirus.

In 'It Is Time to Act', Alice Chudes writes, 'We need to save the planet, / To save *the sacred life*. / There is no time to discuss it! / There is just time to act!'

Countries and cities are locking down their borders, and swathes of humanity are being told to stay indoors. This is the planet telling us to stop, breathe, and respect the balance of nature. In 'A Blessing in Disguise', she narrates: 'Nature seems / To have something to say. / Our planet screams / In its own unparalleled way!'

In 'A Cry of My Soul', Alice Chudes cries to her father, 'You are gone, / Gone with all that you did not say'. Her lines are relatable to many, of course, relatable to me, because we all experience remorse over things we should have said and done.

With her collection of poems, Alice Chudes, like the Phoenix, ensures we will hear what she has to say.

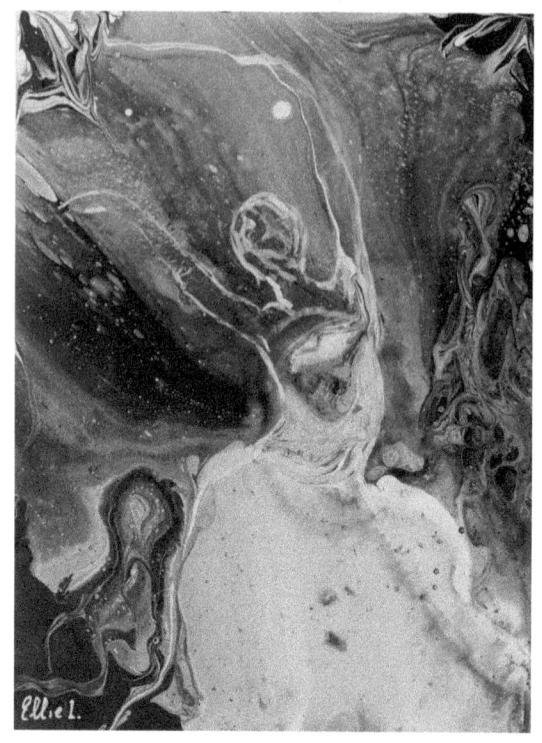

The Nebula Queen, 2017
Acrylic on wood panel 30 by 20 cm
In private collection

All I want is to dance for you and the stars.
—Ellie Lasthiotaki

PREFACE

MY POETRY INTERPRETATION

> No great artist ever sees things as they really are;
> if he did, he would cease to be an artist.
> —Oscar Wilde

While poetry can be very abstract, its understanding is very personal. It really depends on the individual reading it how a poem's verses resonate in the heart based on the reader's life experience.

My poetry does not have an intention to be universal. Rather, it is an expression of my deep thoughts and feelings, which at times can go way beyond *the normal reality* perceived by most people.* I like to bring the reader outside of the everyday life into *the world where just about anything is possible*, the world of dreams, the world where senses are altered, where one can see the invisible forms of light** and discern all the sources of energies around.

I believe there are many,
Not just one, the one people see,
Many realities, many, many,
And dimensions are way more than three.

There are a few ways to connect with this altered reality.

---

* There is a theory that all realities are virtual. Just because most people have the same perception of this reality does not make it less virtual. It is always the matter of optics. All the worlds follow the Heisenberg uncertainty principle that the position and the velocity of an object cannot both be measured exactly, at the same time, even in theory.

** The invisible side of the electromagnetic spectrum.

The first way is through chanting, a sort of *repetitive*[***] singing with a frequent connotation of being sacred. One chants psalms to relate to the Divine, to pray. Whereas the objective of chanting is quite clear, I wish to bring the attention to *the elated state of mind* that one finds oneself in during the time that one chants. While the reality does not change, one's attitude to it shifts as one sees everything in a bright light and becomes more optimistic. It is this fleeting feeling of contentment that one often pursues all life.

Another way is through dancing:

I love dancing in silence
All alone under the stars.

Gazing, dreaming, and laughing,
Repainting in gold all of my scars.

One may refer to the *Sufi whirling* that helps its performers to *transcend into the state of ecstatic trance*. In its essence, dancing is establishing an ultimate connection with the nature, with people around us, and with our own soul. This is why dancing is still used by tribes to transcend into another, outer world, where there are more dimensions than three, and time is relative. Essentially, the soul of the dancer escapes the body and thus becomes for a moment *bodiless*, allowing for a quick transfer of knowledge as the spectrum that one can actually become conscious of suddenly goes to being *limitless*.

There is a danger element in this practice as well. While entering into the state of ecstasy or trance—for those who have experienced this before—is relatively easy, the exit from the parallel reality back into our existence may reveal to be tricky. One might become *trapped*, requiring help to toggle back. Equally devastating are the results of this practice on the energy level, as one comes out totally depleted.

[***] Repetition is often employed in my poetry through the use of refrains: I intentionally repeat a line or a verse, sometimes modifying it slightly, to underline its meaning and to sound like a chorus in a song, which may stay in reader's mind long after closing the book. 'Repetition is the key to changing one's mindset. Sometimes repeating the same pattern can help the mind to clear.' Ellie Lasthiotaki

Speaking about other dimensions, one cannot expect to be born again into a *perfect* reality: a reality where one's life knows no limitations or setbacks. One should aspire to make this reality, the only reality that one knows within one's conscious mind, perfect or as close to being perfect as it can be. In other words, one must do whatever is in one's power to strive to become the best version of oneself here and now. This is the only actual choice that one has, as one cannot influence what happened *already* in the past, and at the same time, one cannot foresee what is to come tomorrow. In other words, life's problems are inevitable and represent an opportunity for personal growth. If one cultivates oneself, one's perseverance, one may overcome all of life's difficulties.

'Eternity I do not need. / I am enough!' says one of my poems. It relates to being self-sufficient. All that one needs for existence can be found inside. Inner peace and harmony with the outside can be attained through self-introspection. It also relates to the circle of life, which explains the existence of infinite space and eternity. One's life as a human being is limited to the space and time that one chooses to be in this world. Yet on another level, all human beings are related to eternity through their immortal souls. Thus, *the finite is intimately connected with the infinite.*

I shall go the roads less travelled.
I shall walk across all the seas.
I shall help those in trouble.
I shall be reborn like *the Phoenix*.

The Phoenix is a mystic bird. She has this outstanding capacity to be reborn from her ashes. People who experienced near-death accidents share the same supernatural power. Both witness a miracle of life that comes back after being nearly extinguished. Both speak of the survival of the human spirit or, shall we say, the soul, which is immortal. People who *believe* (in God, in miracles, in fairy tales, in legends, in rebirth, etc.) have an easier relation with the death. For them, death is the cessation of temporal being. It is *not* permanent as they see another life after their death in this one.

Another wonderful—maybe less known—faculty of the Phoenix bird is that her tears heal the wounds. She lives a very long and tormented life, but instead of becoming embittered or resentful, she manages to open her soul, to make it as pure as the water from a natural source. Her own sufferings make her oversensitive. She feels others' sadness miles away. She is also compassionate and altruistic. She truly wants to help people in their ordeals. This is what gives her this special power to *heal with her tears*. Being reborn after her death, she is *ready to die again* if needed.

The Phoenix did not choose her fate. Rather, her fate chose her. Who else could have done it *if not her*? Let's make a historical parallel with Jeanne d'Arc, who also exhibits a strong faith and relation with God, who acts in his name, and who dies being burned alive. She did not rise from her ashes. Yet what a legacy for all eternity! Ultimately, the *witch-hunt* stopped. Fortunately, we are no longer physically burning those who are *different*. However, in our twenty-first century, women across the world are still not benefiting from the same rights as men. Boardrooms are still predominantly masculine. *#MeToo* is just one of modern phenomena. Today there are still *witch-hunts*: political repressions, racism, ageism, marginalising people with mental illnesses whereas the rate of depression and anxiety in the modern society is flagrant. The fight always begins with just *one person who had enough*, with just one dissident who sets the precedent. More people will follow. In a way, we all have deep inside us the Phoenix bird ready to be reborn from ashes.

Knowledge transpires
Only bit by bit.

Questions force me to grow.
I need to do what inspires,
What germinates
The enlightenment seed.

Children have this outstanding capacity to wonder about things that they see around them, and they ask a myriad of questions to their parents. With the passage of time, however, we tend to forget this sense of curiosity and *live on autopilot*. Hopefully, my poetry can help the adults to remember the children inside them and *to bring them to challenge the status quo*. We absolutely need this ability as a species in order to survive, in order to progress to the next level of development.

Only then we may comprehend
Enigmas,
See the truth behind the mask.

Only then we may awaken ourselves
To connect
Our souls with the infinity dimension realm.

Maybe this eagerness to connect with our own soul and to discover the truth behind the face value is related to *the process of personal awakening*. At a certain point in time, one becomes less satisfied with *one's normal life* and embarks on a journey to enrich one's own existence by transcending to another level.

There is a term in the Akkadian language spoken in ancient Mesopotamia: *Nibiru,* meaning *crossing* or *point of transition,* which is also associated with the equinox and astronomical objects. Such transition is a painful but necessary process on both personal and societal levels.

My love is like an endless ocean,
Ocean of tears, ocean of dreams.
You are my ancient love potion,
My miracle that in silence beams.

I often write about love. As Rumi said, 'All loves are a bridge to Divine Love. Yet, those who have not had a taste of it do not know!' The human being has been created with love in order to love. For me, love is the most absolute expression of being, the purest form of energy in the cosmos, the most powerful force in the universe.

Whatever happened, I love you.
I feel you miles away.
Love is stronger than distance,
    Stronger than time,
    Stronger than anything
    That anybody has to say.

Love's object can be a real person, but love in itself can also be *matterless*. The feeling of love is born and lives in one's soul, elevating it from its struggles, allowing the person to shine as a human being. 'The secret is . . . / You get as much / As you're prepared to give,' says one of my poems. *This phenomenon of being selfless as we truly love another* is definitively an amazing paradigm of an ideal being, or if applied to a wider public, of an ideal society where people genuinely love one another and have a sincere empathy for one another.

Then space, κόσμος,
The universe, the stars,
The explorations,
Trips to the unknown.
Let's find what life's origin is!
Where does it all begin?

The universe and the stars are equally recurrent themes of my poems, since our planet Earth is just a tiny blue dot lost in the immensity of the world, κόσμος in Greek. One of my verses reads, '*"The universe is so big!"* / Said Father.' My vision is that not only are we not alone in the universe today, but also, we have been preceded by many civilisations, on and outside our planet. Nowadays, we are only making the first baby steps into exploring space and we have a steep learning curve ahead of us.

The universe is full of paradoxes, maybe because we do not fully understand it yet. It was my father, a geophysicist at Russian Academy of Sciences, who inspired me since my early age to ponder about it and about our place in it. I am fascinated by the universe, which is infinite yet consists of infinitely small particles, fascinated that *one measures distance in time* that the light needs to travel that distance. Therefore, what one sees through the telescope is a photograph of what happened millions of years ago. This intricate relation between time and space pushes me to believe that neither of them is linear:

Time is never linear.

It is more like DNA.
One spiral to get near.
One spiral to stray away.

Time as a spiral where the past repeats itself over and over again in a different form, on a new temporal parallel, intrigues me. While I do not believe that time travel as related to physical objects is possible, I have a feeling that what is matterless and intangible can actually transfer between different eras.

Next day encompasses
Countless chances.
Yet as time passes,
You realise you travel along
Only one of *the forking paths!*

I look at each and every person in this world as *a sort of a traveller*. One goes from point A, the birth in a specific location, to point B, the death in another location. Each person has his own path. Think of a caravan following Polaris in the desert. However, in my view, every person's *desert* (i.e. the physical space, the location of one's life) and *Polaris* (i.e. the compass or the beacon that one uses to choose one's direction) are individual. We neither move in the same coordinates nor in the same direction; we all have our own unique purpose.

Clouds are also among the recurrent topics of my poetry. They relate both to our world's natural phenomenon as seen from the ground and to interstellar clouds of dust, hydrogen, helium, and other ionised gasses. A *nebula*, Latin for *cloud* or *fog*, refers to a distant galaxy. 'The Nebula Queen', one of Ellie Lasthiotaki's paintings, says, 'All I want is to dance for you and the stars.' In one of my poems, I repeat eight times 'I look at the stars and wonder' to emphasise a mix of curiosity and enchantment with the mysterious, with the untouchable.

I see
    As clear
    As on cloud nine;

Here, the concept of a cloud is related to my psychological state, *my personal nirvana*. It is equally interesting that this poem was written in Jerusalem, in the Holy Land, perhaps the most spiritual place on this planet, and thus inevitably expresses my relation with the Divine.

I thank you, God,

For giving me the eyes
And strength for carrying my load.

I grew up in an atheistic society. The whole country lived according to Karl Marx's statement 'Religion is the opium of the people.' Only some people dared to believe in God and only in hiding, while all others were forced to believe in the personality cult of Lenin, who was considered godlike.

Both of my parents were scientists. I studied in the math, physics, and technology class in high school. This formatted my brain to be on the rational side. Yet from my early days, the unexplainable and the spiritual piqued my interest, and I continually looked for ways to relate to it. My personal path to God has been a long and apparently endless journey:

And I got lost without hope.
For what seemed like forty years,

Today, I believe that the advances in science and technology, our rational side, can be reconciled with the belief in God if we look at the creation of the universe in a broader sense than our planet, and if we consider God as a higher intellect than ours, an all-encompassing quintessence of the cosmos.

I know
    My sixth sense is telling;
I know
    The prophecies are real;
I know
    We've paid enough for the ideal,
    For a peaceful and sinless world.

As far as I am concerned personally, the whole purpose of believing in God is to elevate the human spirit, to unify and to dignify people against their lower instincts. There is not such a thing as a sinless, perfect human being, and at the same time, there are no totally evil, corrupt souls either. We are all shades of grey. However, believing in God helps us to move in this spectrum towards the lighter side of it. Concurrently, if we as humanity manage to unite for *the ultimate good*, using faith as a common support rather than a ground for religious wars, I believe that then and only then can we build *a universal peace* where 'the Earth is full of the knowledge of God', the beautiful future promised in Tanach or the Old Testament.

Moreover, we may think that we have all our time to do that, but recent ecological crises provoked by our careless attitude towards nature make this pivotal shift much more urgent. *It is each and everyone's own responsibility to save the world*, not waiting for any messiahs, and only united, together as a race, as mankind, can we achieve this and build a better world for all. Hopefully, my poetry can be a gateway or an inspiration for people who read it to do just that.

Sunrise is near.
The Saviour is in the skies.
Has always been
With us
Throughout the wars.

He has been here for thousands of years.
No need to look for any more messiahs.

We carry all the light,
The flame, the knowledge,
And the answer
Inside the heart!

Artificial intelligence is our own creation, but as a genie, if released out of the bottle, it can cause, possibly irreparable, damage to our planet and to us. I am far from being a technician or an AI scientist: I leave it to the people well versed in this matter to make sure that it is we, the human race, that ultimately control AI, and not vice versa. Additionally, it is my strong personal belief that one cannot allow AI to read our minds and that we should avoid any devices implanted into our brains.

And that requires courage,
A leap of faith,
Just to believe that you'll somehow manage

To walk
    Until you see the light;

To live
> Until you gain a hope;

To die
> To feel alive;

And to surrender
> To be victorious!

As a closing remark, I shall say that I believe in *the good of mankind*. I believe that, maybe even during our lifetime, we will reach the peace and the rule of righteousness that we have always striven for, from the cradle of our civilisation to the modern age. Maybe we will finally stop destroying our home and stop killing our brothers and sisters.

Maybe it is about time.

About time to embrace wisdom.

For we, which now behold these present days,
Have eyes to wonder, but lack tongues to praise.
—William Shakespeare

Impulse, 2019
From the series of 'Fractured Imperfections'
Acrylic on canvas 92 by 92 cm

A beautiful body perishes, but a work of art does not.
—Leonardo da Vinci

Defining Timelessness

The Need of Spiritual Guidance in Chaos, 2019
Acrylic and silk screen on canvas 50 by 50 cm

Wisdom Is an All-Encompassing Heavenly Ode

Knowing yourself is the beginning of all wisdom. —Aristotle

Let me begin with this:

What is wisdom?

You are wise

When you own the keys
To connect what is random
Into something that isn't.

You are wise

When you can just ignore the noise.
When you follow your gut instinct
Rather than others' choice.

You are wise

When you know that you play just a tiny part
In a worldwide drama
Called God's act.

You are wise

When you can tell the truth from the lie.
When you are righteous.
When your deeds live long after you die.

Consider wisdom as a favour from God.
The perfection of knowledge.
An all-encompassing heavenly ode.

Continued

Continuation

God is unfailingly wise.

From all eternity,
He shows himself in action to us.

We, humans, can't do otherwise.
We need to uncover as much as we can.
We need to act in line with God's plan.

Soaring Spirit, 2020
Acrylic on wood panel 15 by 15 cm

Truth Is What You Hear When You Stand Still
For Jane

Truth is unique, not vague.
You always know the truth using your gut.
Put some light on the spot.
Everything is either true or not.

Why do we need to know the truth?
Don't we prefer life to be smooth?

As attractive as a lie can be,
It is mischievous, can't you see?

A malign allegation without evidence or proof
Can ruin a house together with its roof.
A defamatory attack
Can shatter the person who was struck.

Overcome darkness of history.
Shed some light to unveil
The Divine Truth
Behind each mystery.
Let the righteousness prevail!

Truth in relation to God
Encompasses the world,
Every bit of it, every tad.

It's the gamut of reality,
Which was, is, and will be,
Every joy, every calamity,
Everything that you ever did.

Continued

Continuation

If you are truthful in your heart,
You count your blessings,
Not failures.
And life isn't that hard.

Truth is what you hear
When you stand still.
Don't let what you hold dear
Be dismayed by what you did.

Truth is unique, not vague.
You always know the truth using your gut.
Put some light on the spot.
Everything is either true or not.

Windy Thoughts, 2018
Acrylic on canvas 120 by 60 cm
In private collection

Time Is Spiral Like DNA

The wisest are the most annoyed at the loss of time. —Dante Alighieri

Time is but an illusion.

We have no control over time.
Why do we drink an infusion,
When we can drink a beer with lime?

Time is but a mirage

We want to believe in.
We walk in a desert.
We listen to the wind of change.

Time is but a vision.

The past, the present, and the time to come
Are on a path of collision.
Unrelated time, there is none.

Time is never linear.

It is more like DNA.
One spiral to get near.
One spiral to stray away.

Time floats like a feather at sea

In a fleeting balance
Between what was
And between what will be.

Time is but an illusion.

Reality is timeless.
Can we master our confusion?
No, we are restless!

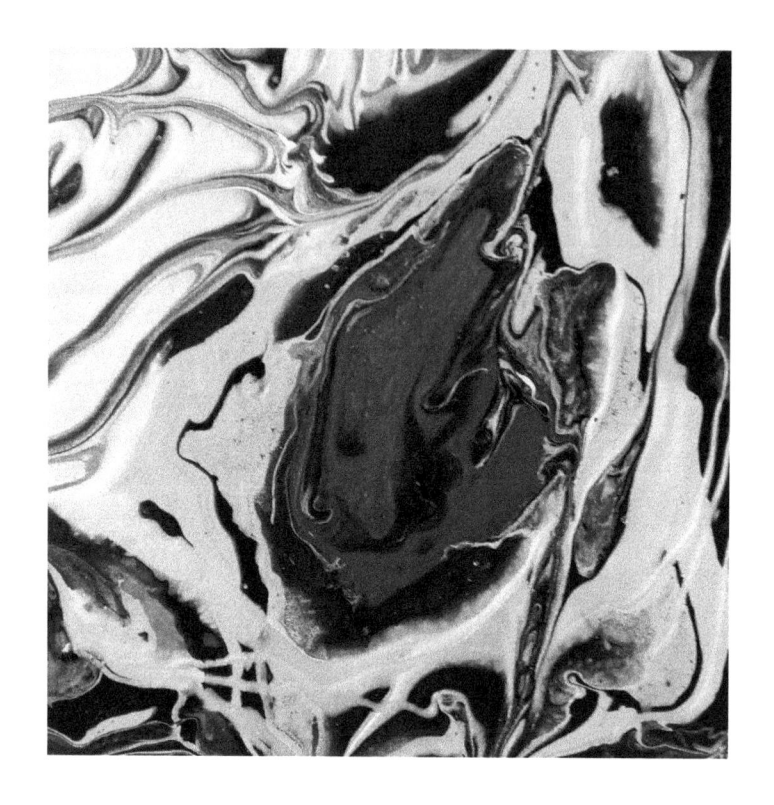

Unearthly, 2018
Acrylic on wood panel 15 by 15 cm

Soul Is an Intangible Quintessence of Life
For Nastya

Quintessence of life,
Immortal, thus sage,
Soul is what guides
From page to page.

Difficult to connect with,
Intangible to feel,
In silence our soul waits
For us to attune to it.

We purify our body
By evolving our soul.
Our ultimate goal
Should be to be reborn.

It is our soul that gives
The first breath.
And when our soul leaves,
The body is dead.

Every day we feed
Our physical form
But we also need
To nourish our spiritual soul.

Both make part of just one.
Coexist in this world both must.

Both define
Human being, dust to dust.

Continued

Continuation

Both *clash*,
As invisibly as they can.

Striving for perfection
At all times, we must be,
We must stand.

Quintessence of life,
Immortal, thus sage,
Soul is what guides
From page to page.

Blossom Study, 2020
Mixed media on canvas 35 by 25 cm

Knowledge Germinates the Enlightenment Seed
For Mathew

Knowledge transpires
Only bit by bit.

How can I acquire
The real sense, very deep?

Without a struggle?
Without investing myself?

Learn to face troubles:
They are the lessons of life!

Knowledge transpires
Only bit by bit.

Questions force me to grow.
I need to do what inspires,
What germinates
The enlightenment seed.

Knowledge is like an iceberg
I can't really catch.
The more I uncover,
The less I can snatch.

Knowledge transpires
Only bit by bit.

The more I learn,
The more I can detach
Away from my doom.

Continued

Continuation

*Everything in the world
Knows only a fool!*

When I meet God,
I am conscious,
There is nothing to hide.
Even if I totally naked
In front of him stand.

It is *the spiritual knowledge*
I need most to thrive,
Raising my soul,
Giving God a high five.

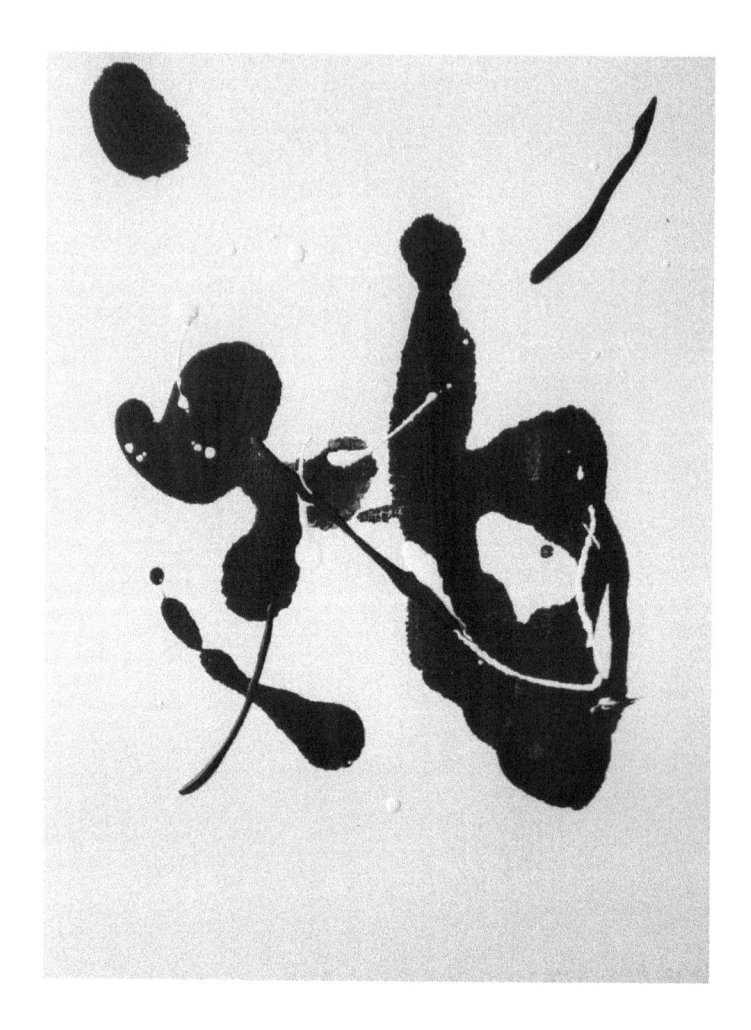

Dispersing Nyctophobia, 2020
Acrylic on paper 30 by 25 cm

Light in a Kaleidoscope Heals in Time of Self-Doubt
Hope is a waking dream. —Aristotle

What is light?

A force dispersing darkness,
A miracle come true each day.
Light makes what's right
To shine with each Sun's ray.

Light brings us precious life.
All in the eye of the beholder,
Light like beauty is yours
And, at the same time, mine.

An electromagnetic wave
That an eye can perceive.
Living beings can be saved,
Can be healed by it.

Light can be clear, can be split
Into colours like a rainbow
In a kaleidoscope
Or on a cathedral wall
Stained glass lit.

Light is energy, its pure form.
The shorter the wave,
The greater the warmth.

Purple, unlike red,
Resonates strongly
With zeal in your head.

Continued

Continuation

Colours speak of emotions.
You say grim to say black,
Depressing, dreadful, ferocious,
Shocking, fatalistic, or dark.

Picture a complete night!
Imagine you know
You will never see light!
If the Sun does not rise,
Think of your fright!

Light is hope.
A silver lining during storms.
When you are in a tunnel,
You need a torch in any of forms!

Light is a telegram sent
Directly from God.
Go, shine bright,
The Divine Light!

What is light?

In time of self-doubt,
In crisis times even more,
Light is what you hope
Against hope for.

Togetherness, 2020
Acrylic on paper 25 by 15 cm

Love Grows the Wings to Touch Infinity

Love insists the loved loves back. —Dante Alighieri

Don't we all live to love?
To love life?
To love
    People?
    Soulmate?
    God?

We learn grammar, math, physics in school
But *not how to love.*
Over sentiments, reason rules.
We are afraid to get hurt.
Petrified to shatter the heart.

So we prefer to hide,
Living life without love,
Doing myriad things,
Leaving what is foremost behind.

We think that love is
Meeting our half.
We forget we are *whole*
Even before we chance on our love.

One plus one
Is not two.
Rather, *infinity.*
Isn't that true?

Love is magic!
Miracles do come true.
Love cures the sick
With the morning dew!

Continued

Continuation

Love grows our wings,
Wings to fly!
Love makes us truly believe
We can finally touch the sky!

We do *not fall in love*.
Rather, we *rise above ourselves*.
Like a newly freed dove
That in air glides hovering high.

Don't we all live to love?
To love life!
To love
    People!
    Soulmate!
    God!

Unpredictability, 2019
Acrylic on wood panel 60 by 50 cm

Life Is a Rose with Thorns
For Rose

In a nutshell, you are born,
You live, you die.

Imagine you took out a loan.
How will you spend it and why?
Isn't it true that each day
You live life on borrowed time?

You surely heard the phrase
'Make each day your masterpiece'.
To invest in yourself pays
Highest interest, loftiest lease.

Life isn't about
Materialistic things.
Clear your head of the doubts.
C'est la vie!
That's what it means!

Take your life as a gift.
And a precious one.
Take only *one* sip,
One step at a time!

Enjoy! Do not run!
Hurrying induces mistakes.
You've got but a lifespan.
Do what it takes!

In a nutshell, you are born,
You live, you die.

Life like a rose has thorns.
You are bound to bleed when you try.

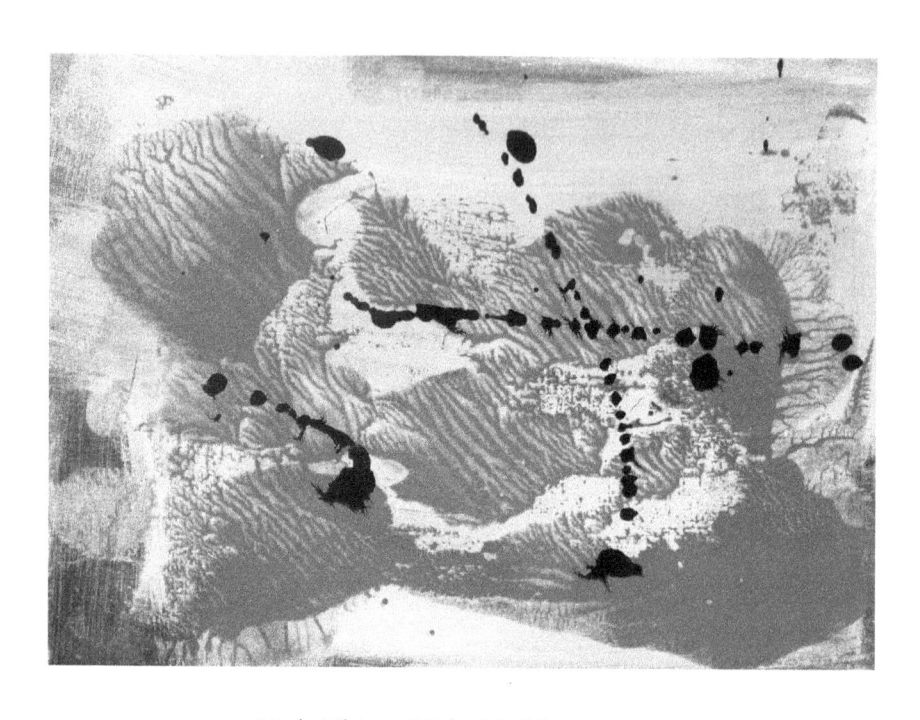

Little Things Make Me Happy, 2019
Acrylic on paper 30 by 20 cm

Happiness Is to Be in Tune with the World
Happiness depends upon ourselves. —Aristotle

At certain times,
Light makes darkness go away.
You breathe full lungs
As you walk, happy under the rain.

You run in a field of wild flowers,
Having switched off your brain.

Can you define happiness?
This is it; I shall say.

You are in love,
In love with this world.
You *are* love,
At peace with yourself.

You hum a merry song
That sings in your heart.
You are happy, happy alone.
You chant and you laugh.

You are in tune,
You resonate at the same wave,
In tune with the world,
You are radiant, you are brave.

Can you define happiness?
This is it; I shall say.

Happiness can't be found externally.
Look inside—my advice, if I may.

I Own My Dreams, 2019
Acrylic on paper 30 by 20 cm

Dreams Are Answers from the Subconscious
For My Mother

Dreams are keys to the lost universe.
Secret coded messages
Our subconscious bursts.

Our dreams are a gateway
Into outer space, back in time.
Nights come after each day
To relax after a steep climb.

A premonitory dream
Comes to those with an open heart.
It is a window into the unconscious realm
Only of a beautiful mind.

Spirits of those deceased
Talk to us in our dreams.
Don't be scared or pleased.
A dream is never what it seems.

Daydreaming is yet another kind.
Building sand castles.
Forgetting life's hassles.
Knowingly indulging own mind!

Visualising is a powerful tool
To achieve what you want in full.

Dreams are useless
One may say.
One synthesises the best
When one wishes to pray!

Continued

Continuation

One receives a dream
As an answer from beyond
While one attempts to bream
One's conscious ship from the mould.

Dreams are keys to the lost universe.
Secret coded messages
Our subconscious bursts.

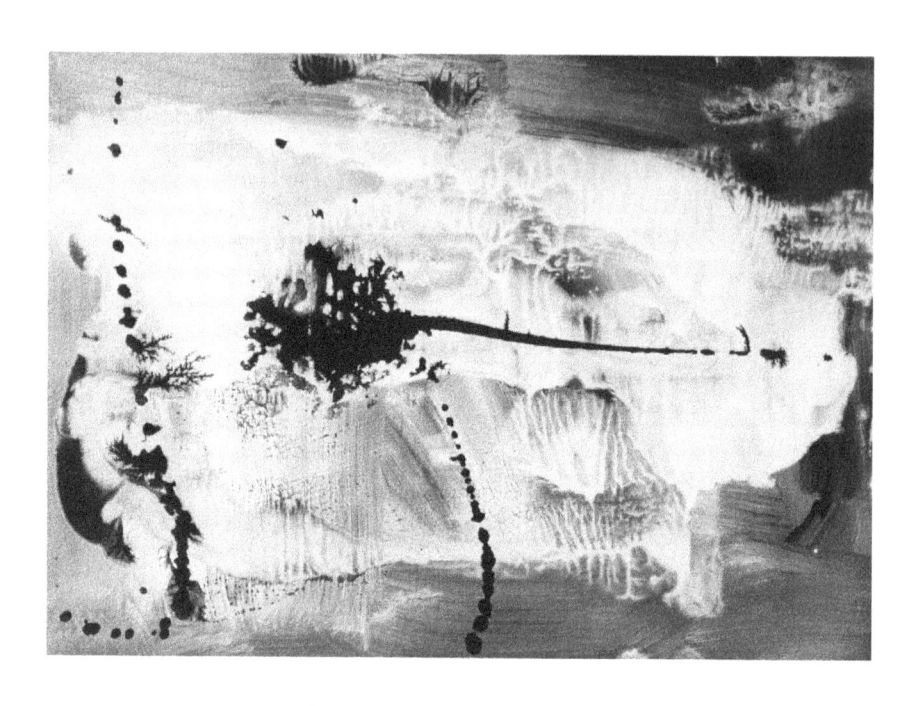

Carving Out My Path, 2019
Acrylic on paper 30 by 20 cm

Destiny Is Carving Out My Path in Poetry
For My Younger Self

Like in stone
Every day
I am carving out my path.

Through my oracle bones
I predict
What is yet to come.

When I take a step
Or I decide to stand still,
I am choosing my way,
Expressing my will.

My destiny contains
All of my steps
Ahead, back, left, or right,
Just like all my breaths
To sustain my life.

Destiny is God's plan
For my lifetime.
Will I be the woman
I was born to become?

People I meet,
Signs on my way
Are all that I need
To discover my pathway.

Continued

Continuation

Call it karma, fortune, or luck,
Providence, kismet, or fate!
I cannot escape the circle of life,
Cannot change my birthdate!

What I can do
Is to leave behind *my words*.
What I write will live on
After my death in this world.

This is my kismet:
To write.
When I do, all my worries just melt,
As my thoughts fly free in the sky.

This is my kismet:
Poetry, prose.
When I do, all my worries just melt,
As I smell the fragrance of rose.

Like in stone
Every day
I am writing my path.

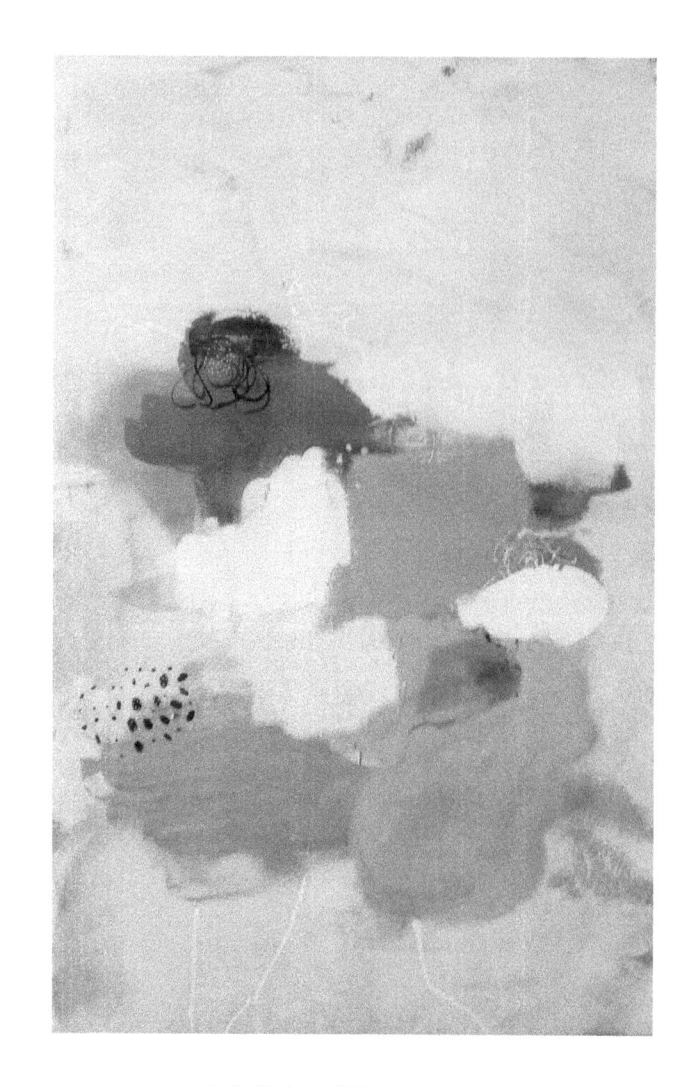

My Echo of Desire, 2020
Acrylic on canvas 90 by 60 cm

Abundance Is Being Wealthy with What Is Within One's Grasp
For Everyone

There is a big difference
    Between abundance and wealth:

Most people pursue the latter, and hence
    Lose their mental health.

One may be wealthy already
    But still think that one needs *more*.

Truth is, one is *not* ready
    To see the abundance metaphor.

Abundance says
    Resources are *not* scarce.

Everyone is infinitely wealthy
    With what one *already* has.

Abundance is a *mindset*,
    Not dull numbers in one's bank.

Tell me,
    Will you really let
        Happiness

    Each time escape your grasp?

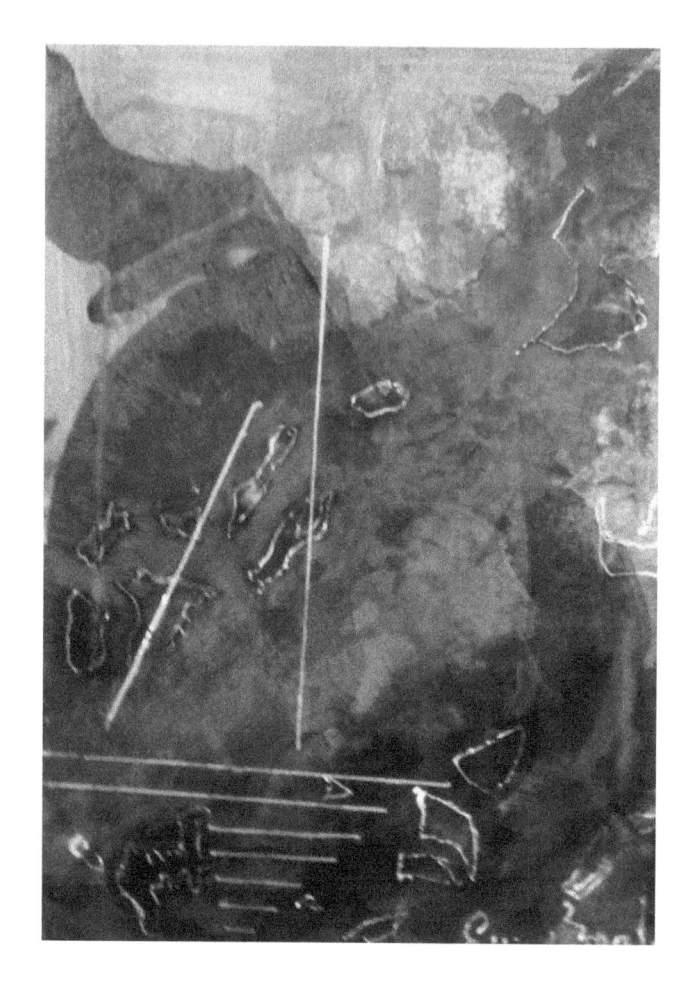

Odysseas, 2019
Acrylic on canvas 30 by 20 cm

> My course is set for an uncharted sea.
> —Dante Alighieri

Phoenix's Saga in Chanted Poetry

2015–2020 Resurrecting Through the Tears of Love

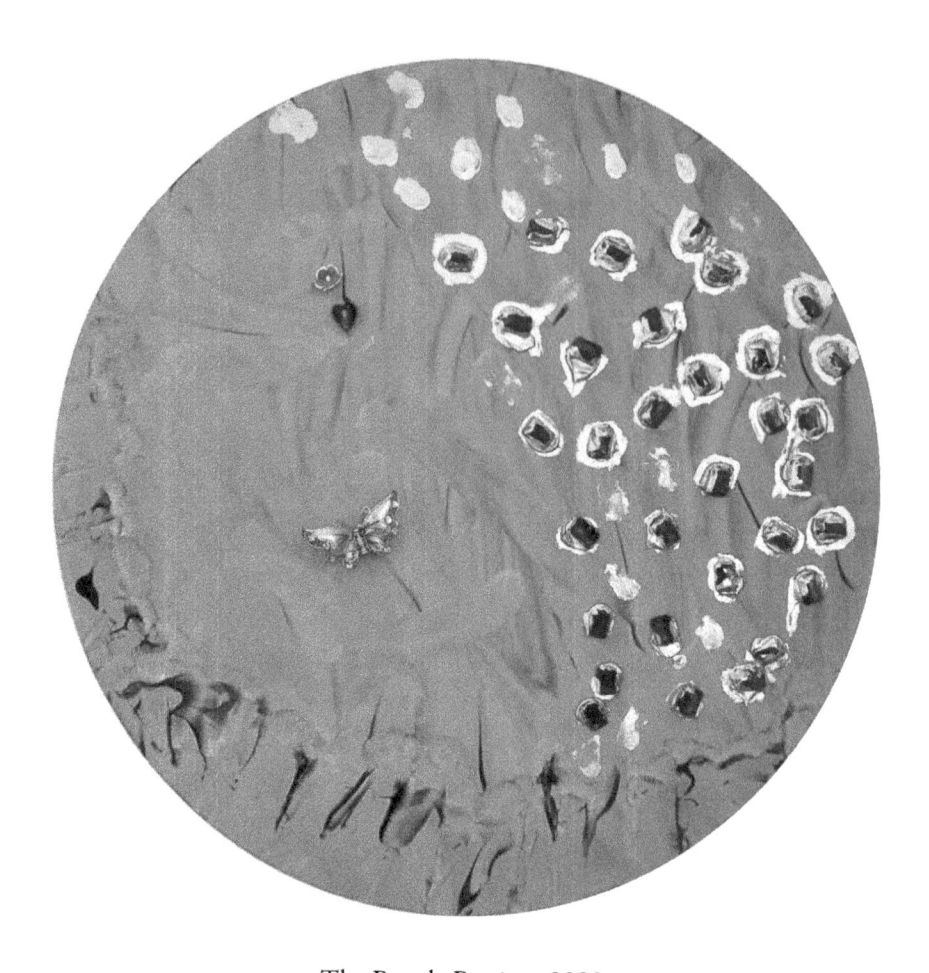

The Purple Passion, 2020
Acrylic and mixed media on circular canvas 50 cm
Illustration by Alice Chudes

> One cannot love and be wise.
> —An English Proverb

31 August 2020
I Saw You in One Wicked and Forbidden Dream
Dedicated to Sergei Yesenin

You had to say goodbye.
    You had to say it – in a hurry!
        Under a stained steel gun
            That was about to violate
                One innocent scalp.

Without *one* single loving soul around.
    Without *one* half-decent word.

I am so sorry that I was not there.
    Sorry, I could not protect you with my own blood!

I am so sorry. Forgive me. I love you.
    Sorry, I could not hold your hand!

I am so sorry.
    Please, do not believe me.
        Do not believe *one* single word that I said.

Do you know that God heard you?
    In the silence of that frozen *Red Moon* night.
        And he heard me crying,
            As I was not able to turn the time… Back!

Our destiny was unfolding
    Without holding *one* moment
        Or *one* inch back.

We were destined to cross pathways
    To exchange *one* single blue-eyed glance.

Continued

Continuation

My dear, I recognised you
    Out of *one* zillion people I met in my life.

We were stolen from spending
    Our lifetime, hand in hand.

Nonetheless, just *one* glance
    Turned out
        To be enough…

Enough to feel;
    Enough to know
        That you were *the One!*

Your eyes were, are and will be
    My Heaven.
        Your spirit still lives
            Inside each *one* of the beats of my heart.

You are my darling, my dear.
    How could I ever forget you?
        How could I ever betray?

All the universe is made of energies,
    Pluses and minuses on one giant ∞D scale*,
        Woven out of variegated shreds
            By *one* high priest to write his Divine Tale.

All the world is but *one* stage.
    All the people are but actors,
        Destined to see but in 3D,
            Thinking there is but *one* right answer.

Continued

---

*   From mathematics, meaning an infinity dimension scale.

Continuation

Invisible things are rare.
    Impossible things are hard to find.
        Everything has always been here.
            Nothing can be made *totally gone.*

Hamsa,
    The invisible hand,
        Is only
            That of God!

Speak to me, dear.
    I can hear you.
        I can hear your heart!

You are my stolen prodigy.
    I saw you in *one* wicked and forbidden dream.

Wait for me,
    Подожди, подожди же ты!**
        I would like to make *one* nice historical film!

Throughout millenniums
    We met countless times!
        And *one* zillion times we missed.

You were in a wrong reality…
    I was in the abyss…

Each time, we were losing precious energy.
    Each time, we were wasting precious time.

Continued

** From Russian, meaning 'Wait for me, please wait!'

Continuation

What to do?
    You are gone.
        I am still here.

What to do,
    Когда ты без вины виноват?***

We were forcibly broken
    Something like *one* zillion times.

Then, *one* heartless sadist
    Glued us
        Piece by piece back.

Glued.
    Only to break again
        And harder!
            Only to kill!

The pain of separation is still palpable.
    I can feel it in each *one* of my joints.
        Yet,
            I am ready
                To die
                      One zillion times over
                For just
            One
        More
    Glance!

*** From Russian, meaning 'When you are guilty, while being innocent'.

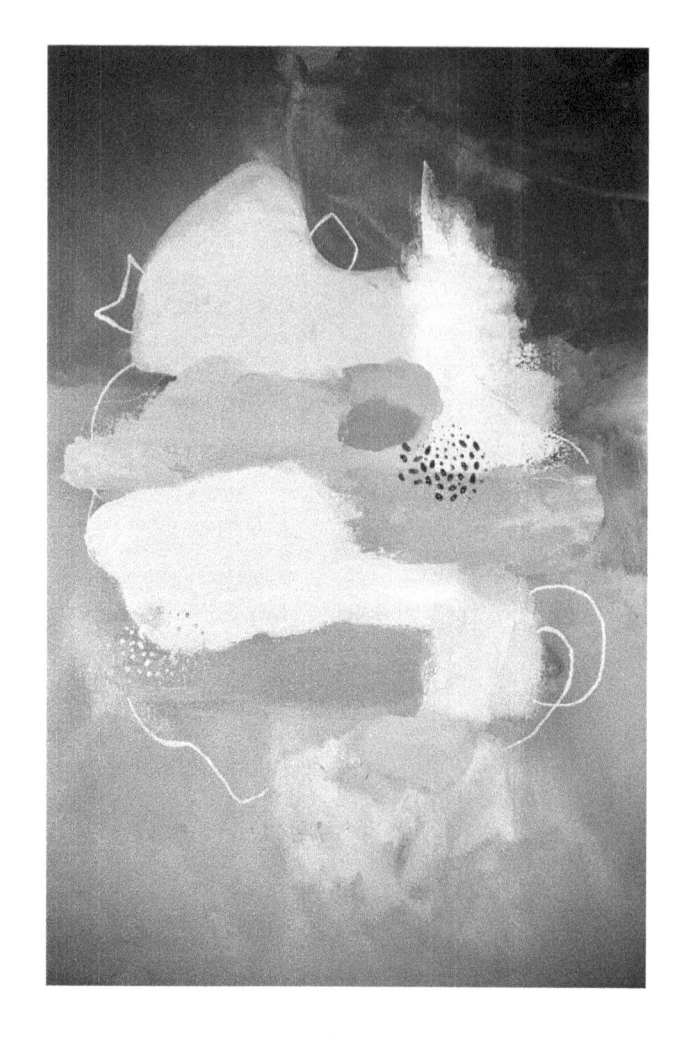

Deep Kiss, 2020
Acrylic on canvas 90 by 60 cm

24 May 2020

*Metamorphosis: Painting the Mandala of
My Past to Release My New Future*

For Myself

I am creating a mandala
To represent my life.

And I am telling myself, 'Brava!'
To encourage my own drive.

It is quite an ordeal
To put all of me on a circular canvas.

And it is a big deal
To portray the sounds soprano to bass:

My joys and my sorrows;
My hopes,
      My deeds,
           My tears,
                My smiles . . .

Each one of my steps that follows
A road into the unknown for miles and miles!

Will I succeed to create a full circle
That paints all that I have seen?

That depicts my nadir and my pinnacle,
As well as all my dreams in between?

Will I succeed to extract harmony
From my chaotic past?

Continued

Continuation

To write an eternal symphony
From the days that turned into dust?

Will I succeed to create
A mandala of my past?

I believe I need to ideate
To build a new future to last!

I believe my zenith
Is within my grasp!

All I need to do is
Let go of my past!

Craving for You, 2019
Acrylic on wood panel 90 by 60 cm

10 May 2020
Truth Is, You Never Left Me
Just for You

Truth is,
    You never left me.
Doesn't matter now
    If you were real
    Or if I dreamt you!

You were there with me,
When I had *no* hope.
You came beaming to see me,
When I struggled to cope.

Truth is,
    You never left me.
Doesn't matter now
    If you were real
    Or if I dreamt you!

I tried to forget you,
    To rid you from my head.
But every time I succeeded,
    I felt *emptiness,* as if I were dead.

Truth is,
    You never left me.
Doesn't matter now
    If you were real
    Or if I dreamt you!

Continued

Continuation

I saw your eyes,
    Saw your face,
Every time I needed
    To feel your embrace.

Truth is,
    You never left me.
Doesn't matter now
    If you were real
    Or if I dreamt you!

You looked at me
    In your dreams.
You talked to me
    When in pain.
Nothing is ever
    What it seems.
You whispered,
    Everything would be okay.

Truth is,
    You never left me.
Doesn't matter now
    If you were real
    Or if I dreamt you!

You were there with me
At my lowest points.
You sent friends to help me
When it seemed
    I had no choice.

Continued

Continuation

Truth is,
    You never left me.
Doesn't matter now
    If you were real
      Or if I dreamt you!

You were there with me,
When I had *no* hope.
You came beaming to see me,
When I struggled to cope.

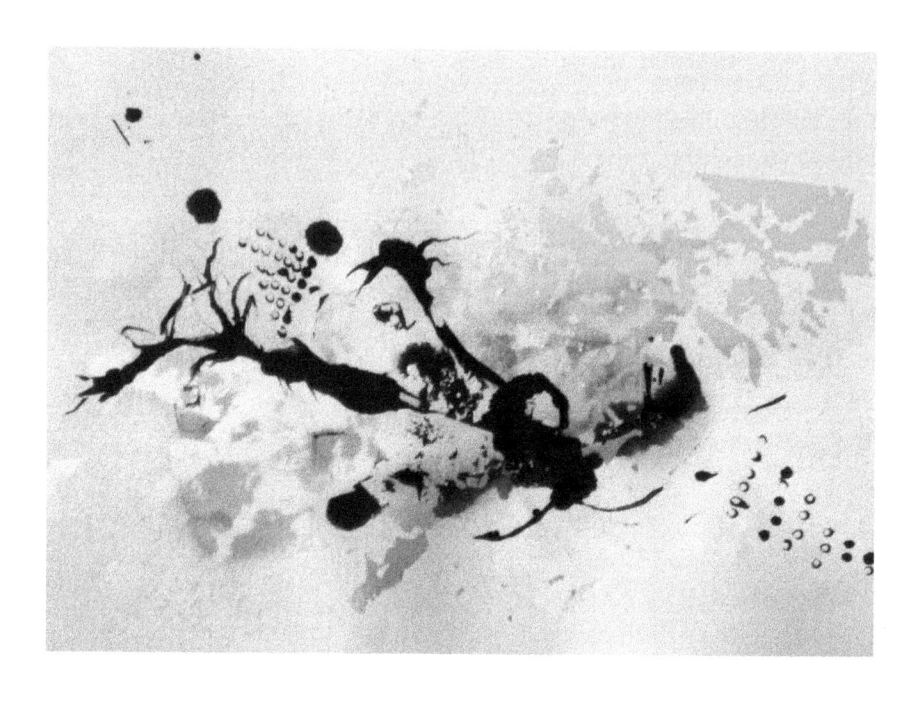

Hidden Letters of Love, 2020
Acrylic and gold leaf on paper 35 by 25 cm

18 April 2020

A Fortune Stroke of Serendipity
Dedicated to My Grandmother

Serendipity, I opened my door!
Life could be gentle,
    Could be like *a fairy tale*.
How could I wish for more?
What else could I say?

I wait for a fortune stroke of luck.
I wait to be swept off my feet.
Indeed, when I met the Tibetan monk,
He told me all that I would need.

He said my future life would be a joy.
Enough of darkness, sickness, and disasters!
He said I could finally enjoy
All that I've built,
    All that I've forecasted.

I think of the monk and smile.
I remember his calm attitude.
His aura was beaming with light.
In an instant, he managed to improve my mood.

Serendipity, I opened my door!
Life could be gentle,
    Could be like *a fairy tale*.
How could I wish for more?
What else could I say?

Reminiscence of Fragrances, 2016
Watercolour on paper 40 by 30 cm

13 April 2020

Ink's Power to Heal

Art washes away from the soul the dust of everyday life. —Pablo Picasso

Poetry for me
    Has a great power to it,
    The power to heal,
    The power of therapy.

When I write rhymes,
When I speak to my Muse,
These are wonderful times
    Of *serenity*,
    Of having *no taboos*.

Paper never complains
    That I said too little or too much.
My Montblanc always remains
    My best friend,
    My best match.

When I put my thoughts, dreams, or feelings
    Black on white,
I am miraculously rescued from the dealings
    That sabotage my life.

Ink replaces
    Any blood to be shed.
Tears I did not cry
    Are capsules inside
    Each and every ink stain.

Art of any kind for me
    Has a great power to it,
    The power to heal,
    The power of therapy.

A Branch of Peace, 2019
Acrylic and resin on wood panel 35 by 15 cm

12 April 2020

My Unicorn at the Genesis of the New World
Just for You

I think of you, my Unicorn.
I think of you today.

You may be dead.
    You may be born.
You may be near.
    You may be far away.

Today, of all days
It is imperative
    To think of *the core*.
Forget all superficial layers.
Think of what matters,
    And then think some more.

These are crucial times.
Times that will show
    Who is who.
Someone's scared.
    Someone cries.
Someone's preparing a *coup*.[*]

Nowadays,
    Everyone has a role to play.
One needs to stay at home,
    To stay safe,
To keep the virus at bay.

Continued

---

[*] From French *coup d'état*, ousting, overthrow, or putsch—the forcible removal of an existing government from power.

Continuation

Despite the crisis,
    Despite what's going on,
I think EQ,
    The best emotional practice,
Is what the world is leaning on.

One needs to resurrect
    From ashes.
Find what one can do
    To help.
Forget old quarrels, conflicts, clashes.
Tighten one's purse and belt.

These are extraordinary times,
The genesis of the new world!
Think of everyone
    Who tries
To stand tall,
    To stand strong.

When the dust finally settles,
When the storm tide goes away . . .

You will receive my letters,
As I dream of you and I pray.

When the dust finally settles,
When the storm tide goes away . . .

There will be cardinal changes,
    As the world betters,
As *love and faith* are here to stay.

Continued

Continuation

When the dust finally settles,
When the storm tide goes away . . .

Everyone still alive will be in fine fettle
And will see
    A better day.

My Unicorn, I think of you.
I think of you today.

Please, stay fit and strong.
I dream I will meet you
    Some day.

Abyss, 2019
Acrylic and Chinese calligraphy ink on canvas 90 by 60 cm

3 April 2020

The Eye of the Perfect Storm

Do not dwell in the past, do not dream of the future,
concentrate the mind on the present moment.
—Buddha

This is the point of no return.

Life as you know it, gone.
COVID corpses to ashes burn.
Nothing that's done
Can be now undone!

This is the point of no return.

Life as you know it, finished.
What lies ahead, can you say?
We all feel smaller, diminished.
We aren't likely to travel in May.

This is the point of no return.

Everyone tries to survive,
Be it a wolf or a man,
No one wants to forfeit one's life.
Everyone wishes to breathe
Time and time again.

This is the point of no return.

The storm is upon us.
We go through a rough patch.
How long can we stand on our own?
How far can we last?

Continued

Continuation

This is the point of no return.

2020, the eye of the perfect storm:
We are trapped, *helpless*, inside.
Everything that was once the norm
Should be from now put on the side.

This is the point of no return.

We hear the thunder as the bubble bursts.
The eye of the storm is such
That everyone simply ignores
What's truly happening inside the crunch.

This is the point of no return.

We came unprepared, without a cushion.
Our hospitals, doctors cannot withstand
Perfect storm's repercussions,
Which as a tsunami go worldwide!

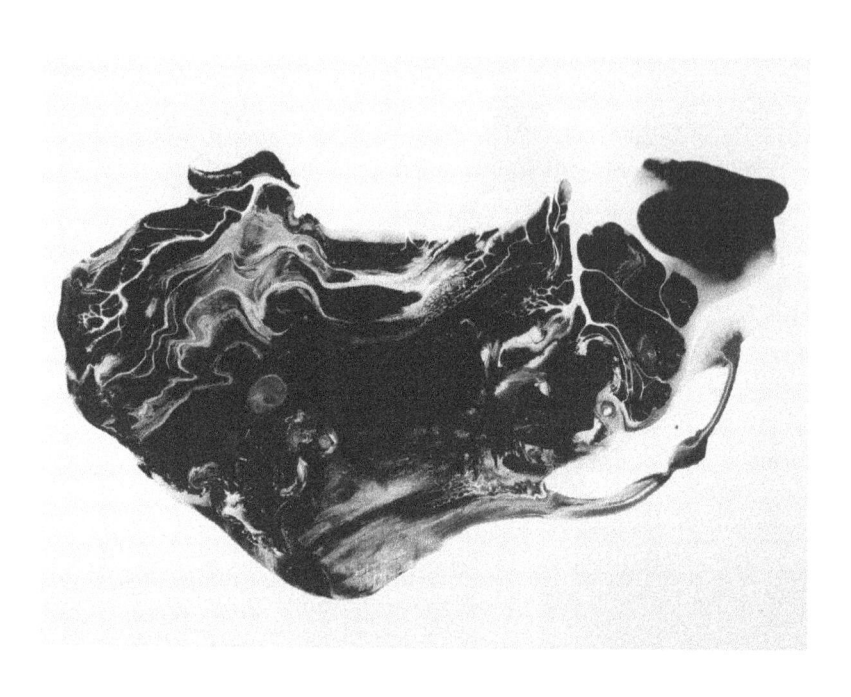

Endoscopy, 2020
Acrylic on paper 30 by 20 cm

22 March 2020
Revelations in Turbulent Times
For Hadassah

What are these
Turbulent times for?

Can you please
Listen some more?

Maybe it is about time
For the Divine Truth
To be revealed to thee.

Maybe it is about time
For the Divine Light
To be perceived by thee.

Revelations come
Only to those,
Only to some
Who don't expect
Them to come.

Maybe it is about time
For the Divine Truth
To be revealed to thee.

Maybe it is about time
For the Divine Light
To be perceived by thee.

Continued

Continuation

It is the way
God chooses to speak.
It is the way
We are warned
For the upcoming trip.

Maybe it is about time
For the Divine Truth
To be revealed to thee.

Maybe it is about time
For the Divine Light
To be perceived by thee.

What are these
Turbulent times for?

For revelations
In psalms and in songs.

Fractured Imperfections 11, 2018
From the series of 'Fractured Imperfections'
Acrylic and gold leaf on paper 15 by 15 cm

> No matter how fractured and wounded
> a human being is, there is always light.
> All it needs is to be perceived.
> —Ellie Lasthiotaki

20 March 2020

Catching My Muse, My Firebird

For Ellie, Anne, Angela, Hammam, Gera, Mathias, Robert, and Vladimir

Who is she? What's her name?
I fear I cannot say!

She comes to me
When I am asleep or awake,
When I am under a tree,
For her or my own sake
She comes to me.

I hear a line in my mind.
I try to catch her tail,
Touch firebird's light
To tell you my tale.

Words are my Legos
To build *a bridge of love.*
Phrases are echoes
Of feelings inside my heart.

She dances my music.
Her lyrics I chant.
With her, I dream big.
Egyptian sphinx is my cat.

Who is she? What's her name?
I fear I cannot say!

She is my mirror reflection,
My shadow on a rainy day,
The other side of a coin.
    She and I are the same!

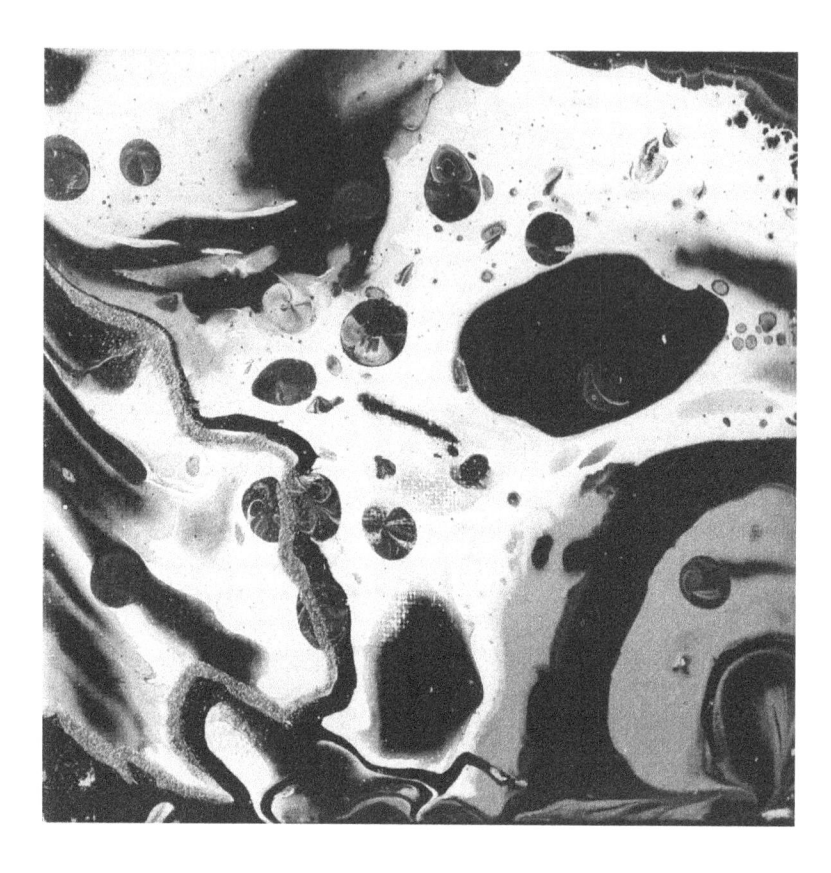

The Magic of the Universe, 2017
Acrylic on canvas 15 by 15 cm

19 March 2020
A Blessing in Disguise
For Inna

I think to myself:
Each situation depends
Solely on one's mindset.
On how one spends
One's days under house arrest.

One may choose to despair:
'It is the end of the world!'
Or one may prefer to repair,
To renew,
    To reconnect,
        To be bold!

Nature seems
To have something to say.
Our planet screams
In its own unparalleled way!

I said this already
And I will repeat:
It is time to act,
Not time to sleep!

So think of it
As of a blessing in disguise.
It is time for us
    To awaken,
        To seek to become wise!

Liquid Gold Duality Defying Rocks, 2019
Acrylic and gold leaf on wood panel 25 by 25 cm
In private collection

16 March 2020
Sacrificial Lambs

The hottest places in hell are reserved for those who, in times of
great moral crisis, maintain their neutrality. —Dante Alighieri

The world has gone crazy
With the global quarantine!
Isn't this disgracing?
What can all this mean?

Like a ghost I walk
In empty city streets . . .
On TV, people talk.
No one extends a hand
When another meets . . .

Some say we came too late
To a worldwide travel ban.
Some speculate,
It's *a conspiracy plan!*

Can't you see?
It's a bloody purge!
The Earth can't be populated by ten billion men!
That's why calamities surge,
That's why bear markets sell.

Virus does not discriminate:
Asian, black, or white . . .
Doesn't need a passport to spread,
Doesn't need a bunker to hide . . .

Continued

Continuation

The new Black Death
Entered the door
With the face of your friend
Or your lovely neighbour!

Do not panic!
Everything is under control.
Stay home if sick.
And take care, LOL.

Can't you see?
We all
    Are
        But
                Sacrificial lambs!
Standing as told
In orderly lines.

The history repeats:
All the same but version two!
The plague is a genocide,
It's God's wrath
For the sins of the few!

A Seed of Knowledge, 2020
Inspired by Alice Chudes' poem 'A Seed of Knowledge'
Acrylic and charcoal on paper 29 by 21 cm

3 March 2020

A Seed of Knowledge
Dedicated to My Grandfather

I last saw you
In 1988.
And it was as if you knew
That it soon would be *too late*.

Too late to talk,
To tell me what you saw,
To say you'll be my rock . . .
What did I need to hear more?

You wanted to groom me,
Teach me how to write.
Without you feels like
I've lost some of my sight.

I was just a kid,
A little girl, eager to learn.
You gave me a gift: just a seed.
And straight after I needed to mourn.

Now a grown young woman,
I remember you as an old man
And I think of the seed,
As I am proud that I managed to grow the plant.

I wish I could know
All that you wanted to teach.
And with a fading sorrow
I could finally reach

Continued

Continuation

Your message,
    What you wanted to say;

And your knowledge
    That I could comprehend one day.

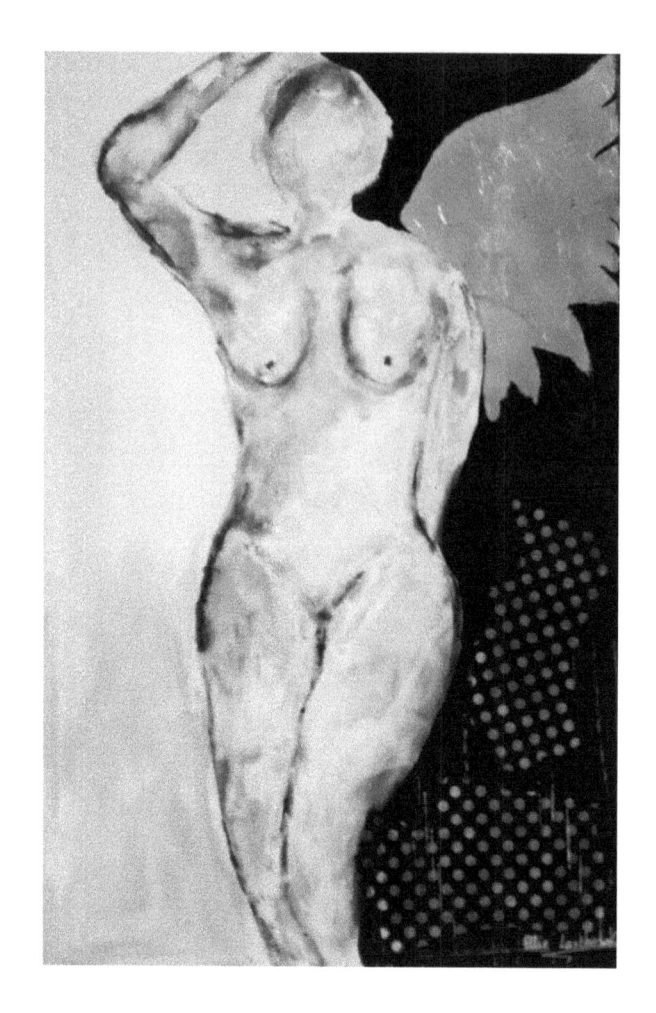

Fractured Imperfections 2, 2018
From the series of 'Fractured Imperfections'
Acrylic and gold leaf on canvas 90 by 60 cm

> No matter how fractured and wounded
> a human being is, there is always light.
> All it needs is to be perceived.
> —Ellie Lasthiotaki

16 February 2020

A Leap of Faith

Dedicated to Jerome Pryor SJ, who taught me Appreciation
of Art in 1998–99 and was a life-long friend

I've taken
    A giant leap of faith
Not knowing
    What lies below
Or what's the length
    Between here, now
And where I am bestowed.

I feel as if I were blind.
Yet God sees for me.
He's really kind.
He truly guides me
When I need it.

I can't *not* be,
Not be whom I'm supposed to be,
Supposed by him,
Not by my own desires.

I write; thus, I am.
To be or not to be
That's *not* the question.
I am not the lamb
Nor seeking another resurrection.

I breathe; thus, I live
Here, today and now.
What trick have you got up your sleeve?
Can you avoid your death somehow?

Continued

Continuation

I've tried to flee,
Not to comply, avoid directions . . .
I shouted: 'I do not want to see!
Don't want more deceptions!'

Yet each time I fought,
Fought with what I need to be,
Each time I got caught,
Reminded to be me,
To be what I am supposed to be,
Not walk the road of the least resistance!

And that requires courage,
A leap of faith,
Just to believe that you'll somehow manage

To walk
    Until you see the light;

To live
    Until you gain a hope;

To die
    To feel alive;

And to surrender
    To be victorious!

Fractured Imperfections 3, 2018
From the series of 'Fractured Imperfections'
Acrylic and gold leaf on paper 15 by 15 cm
In private collection

> No matter how fractured and wounded
> a human being is, there is always light.
> All it needs is to be perceived.
> —Ellie Lasthiotaki

16 January 2020

My Anointed Future

Personality is everything in art and poetry. —Johann Wolfgang von Goethe

Does anybody know
What the future holds?
I'd say the answer's no.
It comes to me and it unfolds
Each day of my lifetime.

I craft my path
One step by one.
Don't do the math!
I haven't won
Uncertainty,
What the future holds!

I wait to see, to feel
How it unfolds.
I can't predict it,
Can I?

The universe is so large!
The possibilities are immense!
I can't see far.
I make each day intense.

And yet I seem to be
At the place and time
That were *meant to be!*
That were *anointed mine!*

Continued

Continuation

I walk, I hear thunder:
'How come?'
I dream and wonder:
'What's the sum
Of probabilities that all are *null*,
Yet equal *one?*'

If it's meant to be,
Then the uncertain outcome
Cannot *not* be,
And therefore, is *certain!*

The probability is *one*.
The way ahead is always *known*.

If I cannot see it,
It does not mean it is uncertain!

Entanglement 1 and 2, 2019
From the series of 'Entanglement'
Acrylic and ink on canvas 120 by 60 cm

Welcome to the fascinating world of entanglement. This is when two quantum particles are highly and intimately connected even when separated by huge distances in different parts of the universe! They are an inseparable whole and react as one to external forces.

A similar type of deep connectivity and correlation is shared between people and events at different points in our lives. Such connectivity makes life itself an inseparable whole.

—Ellie Lasthiotaki

14 January 2020
A Cry of My Soul
Dedicated to My Father

I wish I could call you.
I wish I could hear your voice.
I wish I would see you.
I wish I had now a choice.

You are gone,
Gone with all that you did not say,
All that you've done,
Thought, written, or played.

I wish I could question,
I wish I could ask you about life.
I need a reason,
A motive to continue to fight.

Pensive, 2017
Acrylic on canvas 90 by 60 cm

13 January 2020
#MeToo

Not once, not twice
But many times
I've been surprised,
Misled, embarrassed
By men mistaking me
For someone else,
By them misbehaving!

They can't draw lines
Between what can and cannot be,
Between good old times
When they could do things
And now!

They still get too much *enticed*,
They want what I can't give them!
And afterwards they snatch
As in their eyes, *I am the problem!*

They go crazy, write emails,
Outpour their ego,
Say in court they've done their best
And say *I lied, I just imagined!*

Can they ever stop?
Think with the head!
If they can't behave,
If they can't take a no,
I am not to blame!

They have to realise it!
They have to change
And say that they are sorry.

A Whole Half, 2016
Acrylic on paper 25 by 15 cm
In private collection

6 January 2020

It Is Time to Act

For Greta Thunberg

No great mind has ever existed without a touch of madness. —Aristotle

Go ahead and call me crazy!
I see things you don't!
We can't continue to be lazy.
We need to do what he* wants!

We need to save the planet,
To save *the sacred life.*
There is no time to discuss it!
There is just time to act!

We need to find a way
To understand each other,
To hear what others say,
To care about our own mothers:
They gave us precious life.

It is for us to safeguard it
Against destruction's knife,
Against the jealousy,
Against each other.

As for that nuclear button:
We can't press it!
The Earth is not ours to kill!

The US, Middle East, and Russia
Can live in peace if they only *will!*

---

*   In this context, 'he' means God.

Cataclysm, 2015
Acrylic on canvas 90 by 60 cm

6 January 2020
The World on Fire
For Australia

I see the world on fire.
I see the hell on the Earth.
I can't stop heart's desires
To reach out, to speak with God.

Australia is burning.
Its animals are dead.
While people away are turning
Their eyes together with their head.

They think it doesn't matter
As long as they are safe.
Australia's the first;
They will be the latter.
No one is safe for now!
No one can save themselves!

If people don't help their neighbour,
They will burn us *all*,
One by one to ashes,
Before the Saviour is born!

Circe, 2019
Acrylic on canvas 190 by 90 cm
In private collection

'Circe'*, 2019, was inspired by Katherine Miller's mesmerising story of female empowerment. A superheroine lives for hundreds of years in eternity. She encounters heroes and gods. She creates legends. She learns to use her divine powers, while she comes to understand what it means to be mortal.
—Ellie Lasthiotaki

---

*   Circe (Ancient Greek: Κίρκη [kírkē]) is an enchantress in Greek mythology. She is a daughter of the god Helios and either the Oceanid nymph Perse or the goddess Hecate. Circe is renowned for her vast knowledge of potions and herbs. One of her Homeric epithets is *polypharmakos*, which means 'knowing many drugs or charms'. Through the use of these and a magic wand, she would transform her enemies into animals.

1 January 2020

Six Senses in Jerusalem
Just for You

I wish
> Love was near;

I wish
> My Cloudy dear
> Would hug me soon.

I wish
> He would appear
> On the twenty-second* day.

I pray
> My fate is kinder;

I pray
> The donkey rider
> Is here with us soon.

I pray
> He would appear
> On the twenty-second day.

I see
> As clear
> As on cloud nine;**

I see
> *HaShem* is real;

I see
> He would appear
> On the twenty-second day.

Continued

---
*   Since ancient times, it has been believed that number twenty-two is the number of God, *HaShem*, as well as the number of revelations.

** The phrase 'on cloud nine' is an idiom that means a person is feeling very happy or satisfied.

Continuation

I hear
    Spirits whisper;
I hear
    Signs of the outer world.
    They are very near.
I hear
    They will appear
    On the twenty-second day.

I feel
    The New Earth is coming;
I feel
    Him[***] in my own tommy;
I feel
    A New City will be built.

I smell
    The victory is near;
I smell
    There is no fear;
    Because *HaShem* is in control.
I smell
    He would appear
    On the twenty-second day.

I tasted
    The salt of tears;
I tasted
    The bitterness of sins;
I tasted
    More
    Than I wished for.

Continued

[***] In this context, 'him' means *HaShem* or God.

Continuation

I attest
    We will be delivered
    From our sufferings and death.
I attest
    The end is near.
I attest
    We must fall
    To rise back and higher
    As we've never been.

I know
    My sixth sense is telling;
I know
    The prophecies are real;
I know
    We've paid enough for the ideal,
    For a peaceful and sinless world.

I know
    As a wear
    A seal on my forehead;
I know
    The prophecies are real;
I know
    Not everyone is selling
    One's soul for the gold.

Continued

Continuation

I know
    As I've seen the future,
I know
    As I was told by him,
I know
    He would appear
    On the twenty-second day.

    I even could right now
Touch
    The skies with clouds;
Touch
    The Tree of Life;
Touch
    The Divine Truth.

In Love with This View, 2020
Acrylic on canvas 90 by 60 cm

11 November 2019
Thanksgiving to God

Reflect upon your present blessings, of which every man has plenty;
not on your past misfortunes, of which all men have some.
—Charles Dickens

I thank you, God,

For your protection:
Each step in mud
You guide me in the right direction.

You give me forces
Not to abandon.
You hedge my losses
And you pardon.

Whatever swamp is in my way,
You mark the birches and the moss,
So I would circumvent the mires,
And take the right turn, where roads cross,
And walk in smoke, avoiding fire.

I thank you, God,

For giving me the eyes
And strength for carrying my load.

I thank you, God,

For giving me each grain of rice
And for the light of my Blue Sapphires![*]

---

[*] Blue Sapphire is my birthstone.

Fractured Imperfections 4, 2018
From the series of 'Fractured Imperfections'
Acrylic and gold leaf on paper 15 by 15 cm
In private collection

> No matter how fractured and wounded
> a human being is, there is always light.
> All it needs is to be perceived.
> —Ellie Lasthiotaki

7 November 2019

A Glimpse at Apocalypse

O human race, born to fly upward, wherefore
at a little wind dost thou so fall?
—Dante Alighieri, *The Divine Comedy*

I've seen how it all ends.

Our home, our planet Earth
    Is *lifeless!*

When?
    Less than a hundred years in the future.

We burn it all,
    Destroy to the foundation.

I see the continents
But not the colours.
It went all black.
    A cobblestone!

And there is no way back.
    The game is *over!*

Believe me
    Or believe me not.
    I've seen it with my own eyes!

And I am here to shout *a warning*
To *all* mankind,
To everybody:
'Please, do something,
Do something to avoid it!

Continued

Continuation

No time left for *one* mistake,
No time to argue.
We all are running late.
The train is parting now.
Do what it takes!
Do what you can
To save our home!
This is our very last chance,
    The last lottery ticket.
After it all ends,
There will be none,
No one left.
No Americans and no Russians,
No Chinese and no Persians,
No Israelis . . .
We just kill each other!'

Believe me
    Or believe me not.
    But I have seen it.

Life is a gift.
We owe it to God!

    We don't have the right to void it!
    Don't have the right to kill all living beings!

Life is a gift.
Please use it rightly!

We all are running late.
This is the final game
    But not the rugby finals!

Continued

Continuation

Divide and rule:
That's the Devil's aim.
We play *against each other*.
    Therefore, we are *all losers!*

It breaks my heart.
It skips my mind
Just to imagine
    A *lifeless* planet.

I love so much its beauty!
    And the knowledge,
    The history,
    The literature,
    The paintings:
    All the riches of the peoples of the globe!

And yet
If we do nothing,
Everything just burns,
        Just burns
          To ashes![*]

Believe me
    Or believe me not.
    I saw the end.
    It freezes blood in veins.

I saw it,
Apocalypse's
    Day After.

---

[*] Could we rise from our ashes like the Phoenix bird? Or rather, could we do everything that is in our power to avoid apocalypse while *it is not too late?*

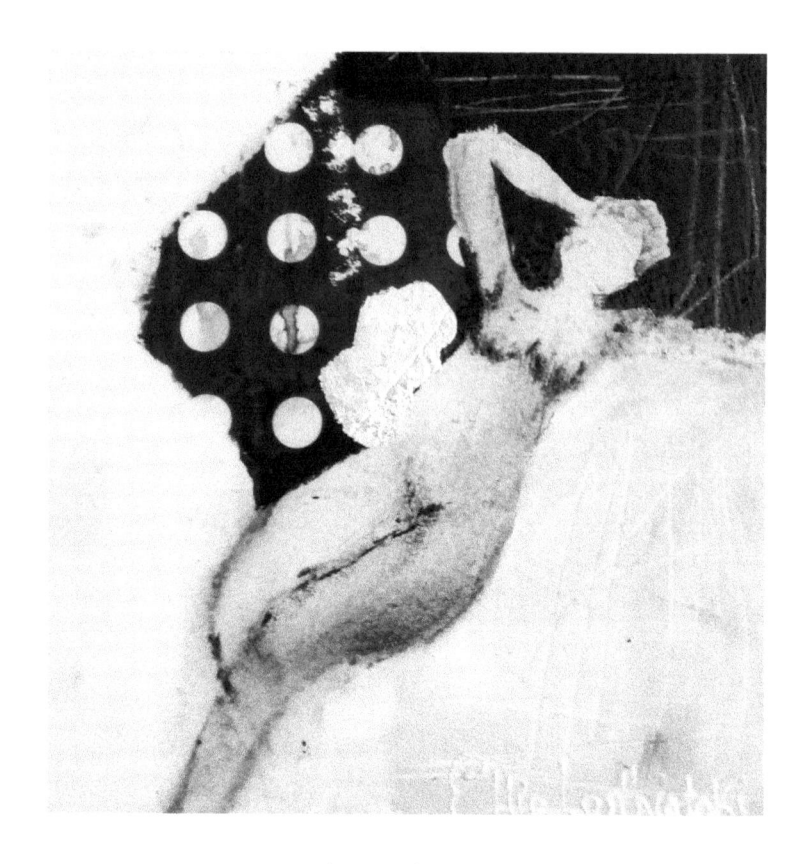

Fractured Imperfections 5, 2018
From the series of 'Fractured Imperfections'
Acrylic and gold leaf on paper 15 by 15 cm
In private collection

> No matter how fractured and wounded
> a human being is, there is always light.
> All it needs is to be perceived.
> —Ellie Lasthiotaki

6 October 2019

A Message in a Bottle

Love, that moves the Sun and the other stars. —Dante Alighieri, *Paradiso*

I met you, it seems
In another life.

Your and my existence
Are parallel or alike.

When I saw you,
I knew at the spot,
Our love wasn't new,
We never put the dot.

Yet some malicious forces
Keep us apart.
They tell you untrue stories
And break, tear up my heart.

I haven't seen you
For an eternity now, it seems.
It's like I dreamt you;
You never lived here; you don't exist!

I am not ready
To wait for you for another life.
I wish you heard me already.
I don't want to waste our lives.

But how can I connect the dots
That are floating in parallel worlds?

I send you my fondest of thoughts.
Find me through the web of roads!

Continued

Continuation

I'll be waiting for you.
I've been waiting for thousands of years.

Find me!
It's true:
I'm yours
    And can't be anybody else's!

Tornado, 2018
Acrylic on wood panel 50 by 50 cm
In private collection

26 September 2019
Lost Without Hope
For Those Who Seek the Way

I can't live like others.
I need different things from life.
My heart in silence suffers
As if it were under a knife.

As if someone had poisoned
My daily tea, my daily path,
I walk like in a war zone,
From worse to worst to bad.

Only at night, I let me dream.
I close my eyes to find the peace.
Nothing is what it seems.
A lonely star inside the mist.

I have done wrong, too many times.
I haven't seen behind the mask.
I have written prose without the rhymes.
I drank instead of filling up the flask.

And I got lost without hope.
For what seemed like forty years,
With no camel, just a goat,
With torch for light and boots to wear,
I guess it wasn't bad at all.

I wasn't guiding anyone behind.
Yet I was seeking, searching
Things that obviously I couldn't find.
Things that need researching.

Continued

Continuation

One starry night four years ago
I came to where I belong.
I knocked, but they said no.
I had to leave but not for long.

From then, it doesn't really matter.
I know where home is.
A place, a people? Yes, the latter.
I found them. They found me.

And even if I don't speak the language,
I feel I am on the right way.
I don't know all the answers
But I do know what to say.

No one said that it'd be easy.
No one flew outside the Milky Way.
Everyone is just busy
To make it through another day.

And here I am with all my nonsense.
Seeking the truth, longing for peace,
Peace without borders and fences,
Planting Garden of Eden bis.

I feel different yet not alone
Like I have been before.
And with no answer, I phone
SOS text. What do you want more?

Yet my beacon of hope is back.
Now I know, you hear.
My people have now my back.
Question of time, my dear,
Question of time, you'll come back.

Fractured Imperfections 6, 2018
From the series of 'Fractured Imperfections'
Acrylic and gold leaf on paper 15 by 15 cm
In private collection

> No matter how fractured and wounded
> a human being is, there is always light.
> All it needs is to be perceived.
> —Ellie Lasthiotaki

11 July 2019
My Outside-the-Box Mantra
For My Mother

I refuse to conform to a box.

'This is good. This is not.
Do not think for yourself.
Assemble the wealth.
Best is to store value in gold.
March in line.
Think what you are told.'

I refuse to conform to a box.

I see value in feelings,
Relationships, soul's warmth.

I see colours not in shades of grey
But in shades of the Sun,
As a rainbow,
A beautiful rainbow, man!

I assemble ideas, experiences, trips,
And I store fond memories, stories of these.

I refuse to conform to a box.

I never march by an order—
I'd rather die!—
I wander, marvel, and at times, fly.

Continued

Continuation

I spend my days and nights
Thinking what it would be like
If people did indeed have equal rights,
If people cared, *if we were wise.*

I believe there are many,
Not just one, the one people see,
Many realities, many, many,
And dimensions are way more than three.

I believe the past, the present, and the future
Are intertwined indeed.
How? Through soul's connections
Via thoughts, visions, and dreams.

The *déjà vu*, the sixth sense,
Is a warning from the future,
A telescope with a broken glass lens.

Now, how to connect the dots?
Enter into a trance to transcend—
Wait, and go back? Antidote?

Only then we may comprehend
Enigmas,
See the truth behind the mask.

Only then we may awaken ourselves
To connect
Our souls with the infinity dimension realm.

Continued

Continuation

There, knowledge is infinite,
Light is like a torch,
Ultimate wisdom awaits
Those who dare approach.

Adam's apple was fake:
God would have never
Punished mankind
For its own sake,
For wanting to grow, to learn,
To step into the unknown
Using its brain.

What is true, on the other hand,
The brain is like a muscle
We need to train,
Train up the mind
For the good of mankind.

We need a base for each level of knowledge:
Math fractions
For Golden Ratio to be seen,
Applicable in many interactions,
Music, painting, architecture,
And all other arts, on which we are keen.

We are given only what we can see.

We cannot skip any levels—
It's like Mario Game—
The knowledge in levels is capped by him*.

Continued

---

*   In this context, 'him' means God.

Continuation

We read a book,
Which we need to rewrite.
Yes, the book with pages erased
That we bring back to the light
By advances in science
One page at a time
Over thousands of years
Through enlightenment and sometimes the defiance,
We rewrite the forgotten over the years.

This is why light and knowledge
Transcend only bit by bit.
It requires courage
To stand alone against all the myths.

Enigmas, once understood,
Will be just garbage for someone
Who did not interpret them,
Who is *still in the woods*.**

Put in plain language
The message is only as good
As the interpreter's will
To explain
For it to be understood.

We as a race
Still have a world to learn.
When we move into space
Then we might fly,
Only after we fall.

Continued

** 'Still in the woods', as opposed to 'out of the woods', meaning being out of danger or difficulty.

Continuation

We are given only what we can see.

Knowledge exists already.
Study the science,
Awaken your senses,
For it to be revealed to thee!

Blossoming Truth, 2019
Acrylic on canvas 25 by 25 cm
In private collection

4 July 2019

Truth Always Leaks Out
For People Fighting Defamation

Truth is like water.

Supressed for many years
Underground, it got to
Leak through the layers
To be uncovered to the public,
To be revealed.

Truth is like water.

No matter how secret,
One day, someone wins the lotto
Stumbling upon it,
Making it revealed.

We live in the world of spying.
Hide and seek on a global scale.
Why do we need more people dying?
Shouldn't the liars be ashamed?

Defamation, slander,
How can people use
As a common currency?
In place of the real news?

Maybe I am an idiot,
A naive girl in a nasty world.
I just think lies are hideous,
Destroying people with integrity,
Putting first money, gold.

Truth is like water.

Supressed, it got to be revealed.

Devoted Dreams, 2018
Acrylic on canvas 90 by 60 cm
In private collection

Secret, parallel lives, worlds here and there, places we lived, memories, reminiscent voices of people we met, loved, dear voices… Then we lose them, but the sound of their music has left a trace in our minds, thoughts, subconscious.
—Ellie Lasthiotaki

14 June 2019
A Sight of the Parallel World
Life is really simple, but we insist on making it complicated. —Confucius

I dreamt of you.
I dreamt today.
I dreamt you knew
And came my way.

I saw your eyes.
I heard your voice.
We both knew what were the lies
And we could talk and talk, rejoice.

A dream is a dream,
A parallel world.
Nothing is what it seems.
Reality is heavy, cold.

Yet each day, each dawn
I dream it'd be *the day!*
So my heart can go on,
I walk, I hope, I pray

    Each day,

        Each day . . .

I Am Enough, 2014
Acrylic and pastels on paper 20 by 15 cm

11 November 2018

A Hymn for My Subconscious Mind

We know what we are, but know not what we
may be. —William Shakespeare

Eternity, I do not need.
I am enough.

To all who listen
I shall speak;
To all who whistle
I shall chant;
For those lost
I'll light the path;
As for the ghosts,
I'll solve the math
On how to communicate
Between the worlds,
Between the stars
That blink at night
But died billions of years back.

Eternity, I do not need.
My life's enough!

The hungry I shall feed
And soothe the cough
Of those sick.

Eternity, I do not need.
I am enough!

Wild Thoughts, 2018
Acrylic on canvas 60 by 45 cm

30 October 2018

I Wish I Were Not Alone

Dedicated to My Grandmother

I wish I were not alone.
I wish it were not true.
I wish I could better cope.
I wish I could go through.

What to do? What to say?

When you are not believed?

What to do? What to say?

When it seems that you have never lived?

When people say it's a lie,
And when all you want to do is to cry?

I wish I were not alone.
I wish it were not true.
I wish I could better cope.
I wish I could go through.

What to do? What to say?

When you are blamed?

What to do? What to say?

When you are told to be ashamed?

I wish I were not alone.
I wish it were not true.
I wish I could better cope.
I wish I could go through.

E-motions, 2019
Acrylic on canvas 90 by 90 cm

Emotions are energy in motion.
—Ellie Lasthiotaki

6 October 2018

A Million Shattered Pieces

Love is holy. —William Shakespeare, *All's Well That Ends Well*

My heart has been broken,
Has been shattered apart
Into a million pieces,
Which were never glued back.

Over the years
My soul has cried
A sea of my tears,
A sky of my sighs.

I had to keep walking,
I had to withstand
Whatever life battles
Were still in front.

My heart has been broken,
Has been shattered apart
Into a million pieces,
Which were never glued back.

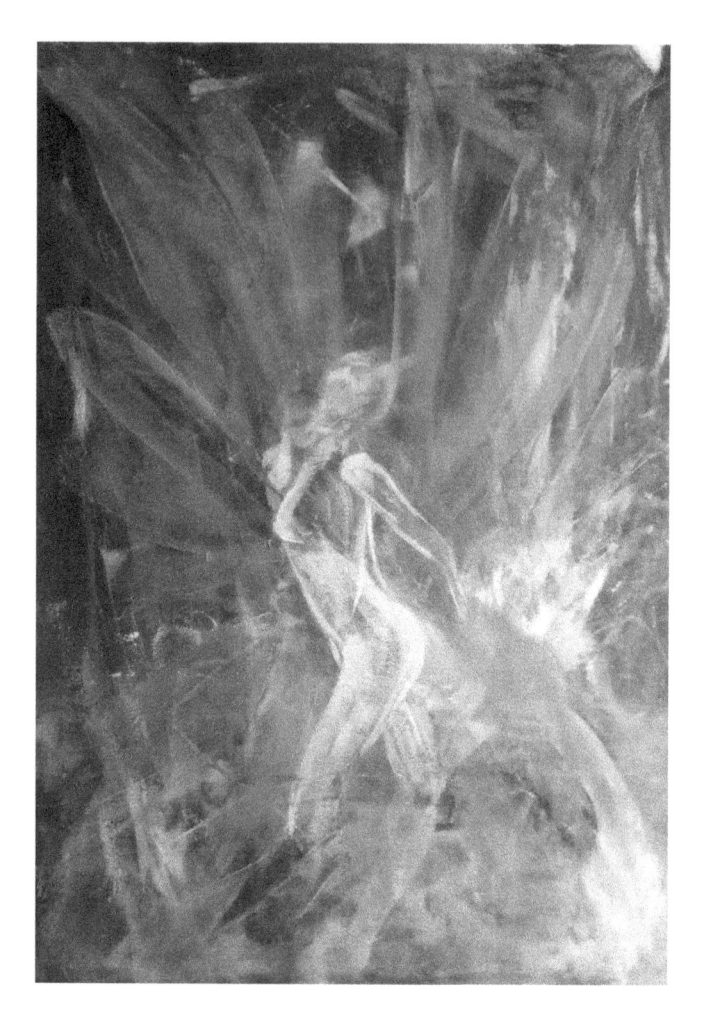

A Chanting Phoenix, 2020
Acrylic on canvas 60 by 40 cm

1 September 2018

Walking in Your Footsteps
Dedicated to My Father

You and me, we are always together.
You and me, we will go far.
I am walking in your footsteps forever.
I have washed away all the tar.

I am free and I am not scared,
Not scared to die, not scared to fight.
I got trained, got prepared
To jump on an ultimate flight.

Things might get complicated.
Things might get even messed up.
But who cares? I am dedicated
To make things this time right!

I shall go the roads less travelled.
I shall walk across all the seas.
I shall help those in trouble.
I shall be reborn like *the Phoenix*.

I am against the destruction:
'Мы разрушим
    До основанья, а затем. . .'*
Let us start with the construction
Of world peace on the planet *Zen!*

Continued

---

* A line from the Soviet hymn in Russian, saying, 'We will destroy everything until the foundations, and only then . . .'

Continuation

There are many who will try to stop us.
They will lobby everything against.
But have no worries, trust me,
Our word will be proclaimed!

This is just the nature,
Black and White,
And *the eternal fight,*
Ever since our creation,
Ever since we saw the light.

No one is bad forever.
No one is good all life.
When in doubt, stick together,
Choose what's right,
And aim above!

Be an eagle. Be a tiger.
Fly not to the Moon but to the stars!
Be a dreamer! Be a writer!
Write your own life and have the guts!

Wine Bottle Study, 2016
Watercolours on paper 25 by 20 cm

15 February 2018
The Secret Love Potion

Nothing that you have not given away will ever be really yours.
—C. S. Lewis, *Mere Christianity*

Don't close your eyes
To dream of love.

It might suffice
To open your heart,
To let it beat
As fast, as strong
As it would want it.

You might be wrong.
You might be right.
Don't put up a fence.
Don't try to hide.

The secret is,
You get as much
As you're prepared to give.

Shallow streams,
Shallow hearts
Don't fill big dreams
And don't give a chance
To conquer the world
Of love and romance.

On the palm of your hand
To your love bring your heart.
If you're destined to be,
Conflicts like clouds will part
And *I* shall turn into *We.*

Continued

Continuation

The secret is,
You get as much
As you're prepared to give.

Do not be afraid.
Do not give up.
You'll recognise your half,
When you cross his or her path.

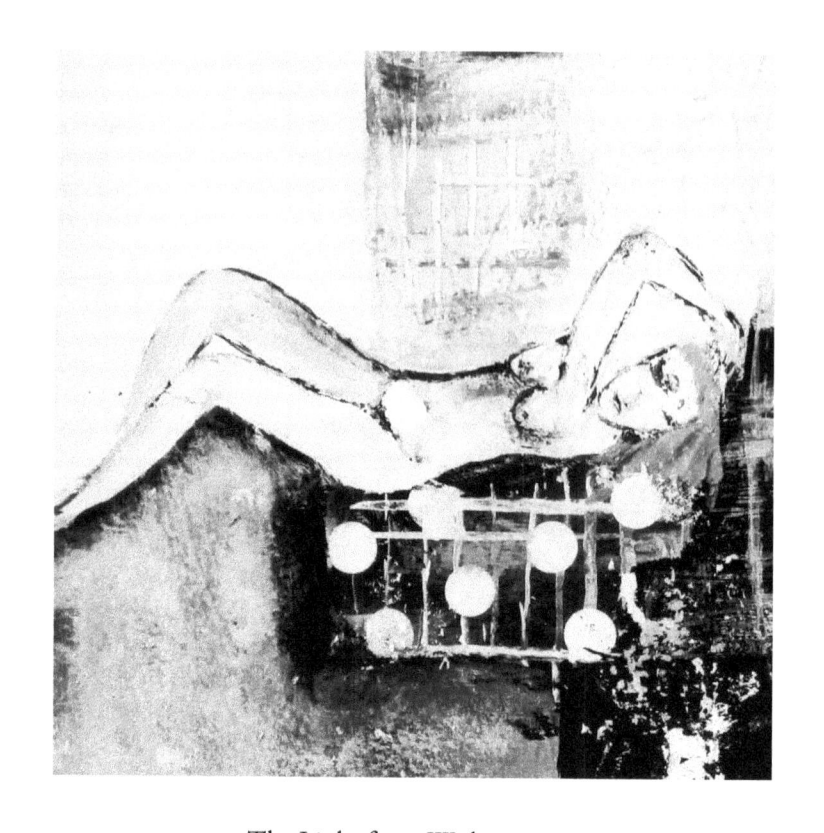

The Light from Within, 2018
From the series of 'Fractured Imperfections'
Acrylic and gold leaf on paper 15 by 15 cm
In private collection

> Sometimes external sources bring light.
> Light is an essential component of existence.
> Blessed are the ones whose light shines from within.
> —Ellie Lasthiotaki

18 September 2017

I Wander, I Wonder, I Speak to the Stars
Wisdom begins in wonder. —Socrates

I look at the stars and wonder,
Where, which one did we come from?

I listen to rain and thunder
And dream about ancient Rome.

I use morning dew as a mirror
And I love listening to birds' songs.

I like to get lost in forests and meadows
Rolling in grass, breathing full lungs.

I love dancing in silence
All alone under the stars.

Gazing, dreaming, and laughing,
Repainting in gold all of my scars.[*]

I would fly on the Venera[**]
Tomorrow if I only could.

And I would change it forever,
Bringing life back as I should.

Continued

---

[*] *Kintsugi* (金継ぎ, 'golden joinery'), also known as *kintsukuroi* (金繕い, 'golden repair'), is the Japanese art of repairing broken pottery by mending the areas of breakage with lacquer dusted or mixed with powdered gold, silver, or platinum.

[**] The Venera (Russian: *Венера*) program was the name given to a series of space probes developed by the Soviet Union between 1961 and 1984 to gather information about the planet Venus.

Continuation

I look at the stars and wonder,
Where, which one did we come from?

I look at the stars and wonder,
Where are you, my love, and when do you come home?

Meeting you was written long before we were born.
All my life was destiny unfolding on its own.

I look at the stars and wonder,
How can we change this world?

How can we create a worldwide garden?
How can we break the mould?

I look at the stars and wonder,
Where to find the key

That will open all secrets
And unlock all chains on the trees?[***]

I look at the stars and wonder,
How to build a better world?

Continued

[***] Makes reference to Alexander Sergeevich Pushkin's poem 'Ruslan and Ludmila' in Russian:

У лукоморья дуб зелёный;	On seashore far a green oak towers,
Златая цепь на дубе том:	And to it with a gold chain bound,
И днём, и ночью кот учёный	A learned cat whiles away the hours
Всё ходит по цепи кругом.	By walking slowly round and round.

Continuation

How to break Babylon Tower?
Where to go, not to be sold?

I look at the stars and wonder,
What can I do? What can I do today?

Dawn is upon us.
Light is here.

Just take your phone
And call to say, 'Hey'.

I look at the stars and wonder,
Is it really true? Did we make it?

Is the storm over?
Or should I still die for you?

Dawn is upon us.
Light is here.

This means,
It is a new day.

The day to create all over
Under the Sun's first ray!

Self-Portrait, 2018
Acrylic on canvas 20 by 20 cm

13 August 2017

A Weeping Soul in the River of Life

Three things cannot be long hidden: the Sun,
the Moon, and the truth. —Buddha

Torn apart and spit upon,
Stained with blood,
Tormented, tortured.
Pinned with *Hedgehog Gloves*[*]
And labelled *worthless*
Russian Soul is.

The tsar is no more.
The new tsar is here.
The River of Life is torn.
Torn down by fear.

A hundred years of violence.
A hundred years of hatred.
A hundred years of tears.
A hundred years of terror.

An innocent was thrown into prison.
His wife wrote letter after letter.
Her brother found a reason
Never to answer.

A monument was raised
In memory of the brother,
The communist leader,
Who died in bed
Long, long after
The husband had been shot dead.

Continued

---

[*] 'Hedgehog Gloves' refers to Nikolai Yezhov, Chief of N.K.V.D. in the times of Great Terror of 1936–1938 in the U.S.S.R.

Continuation

Accused, therefore guilty!
A traitor,
An enemy of the state . . .
Now, can you please tell me
Who actually the traitor is?

But driven by fear,
Fear for his own life,
Can we blame the brother
That he had closed his eyes?

The Perfection of Nothingness, 2019
Mixed media on canvas 90 by 60 cm
In private collection

The first impression triggers curiosity, which forces us to dive deeper in what is seemingly out of our comfort zone. Fuelled by the duality of our inner inadequacy and at the same time the certainty that we can pull through, we proceed to the next level filling some of the void and reaching the first level of emotional understanding.

In the next level, emptying ourselves from experience and known emotions, we can progress to the territory 'nothingness', where lots of wonderful magical things can happen. We can explore these worlds only from afar, internally and externally, as we visualise being in that beautiful moment of feeling and doing nothing.
—Ellie Lasthiotaki

27 April 2017
An Illusion of Separation

It's not what happens to you, but how you react
to it that matters. —Epictetus

I know I should forget you.
I know I should say bye.
And probably I should let you
Live without love or die.

I do go crazy
When somebody mentions your name.
And some part of me knows
That you do exactly the same.

We all meet many people
Passing through our lives.
Yet there are few, just a little
Who stay and do not just pass by.

Chance, destiny chose
To put you on my way.
It is up to you now
How to behave, what to say.

I can't love you forever
Without you loving me back
And yet I can only see us together
Since I can't bear being apart.

I have this dream or illusion
That one day I'll hear your voice.
You will call me to say you love me
And you will hear my tears' noise.

Continued

Continuation

I will fly to meet you wherever,
And you will be in the airport.
You and me now together,
Eye to eye, hand in hand.

Strangers, 2015
Acrylic on paper 20 by 15 cm

14 April 2017
Two Acquainted Strangers
Life without love is no life at all. —Leonardo da Vinci

One moment, one second
I saw you by chance.
Enough to unsettle
Brittle peace in my heart.

No hellos, no smiles exchanged.
We are strangers.
How did we get to this?

Whatever happened, I love you.
I feel you miles away.
Love is stronger than distance,
    Stronger than time,
    Stronger than anything
    That anybody has to say.

Trust me, I forgave you.
Forgave you for good.
And I feel you forgave me,
Forgave as you could.

Beyond Senses, 2018
Acrylic, oil, inks, and pastels on canvas 90 by 60 cm

> I am more than you can see,
> I am more than you can feel,
> I am more than you can smell,
> I am more than you can touch,
> I am more than that . . .
>
> I left my body outside and got in with just my mind.
> —Ellie Lasthiotaki

17 February 2017

A Medium in Love
Just for You

I feel you.
    You are in pain.
I'd love to hold you
    And tell you it's OK.
Rumour has it
    That you even changed your name.
A friend of a friend said
    You don't look the same.
I had nightmares,
    I could not sleep.
You were there with me.
    Under my skin very deep.
I was troubled, unsettled
    But not deceived.
Your voice I would recognise
    In a billion people I meet.
Your eyes are my Torah,
    My ocean, my light.
Your brain is still sharp
    And extremely bright.
I would have so much liked
    To have you back as my boss.
Our fight is our biggest
    Mutual loss.
Your advice would have been
    Priceless for me,
As I am running my own business,
    Fundraising as I had done for thee.
I miss you like crazy.
    And I want you even more.
Please come to find me.
    I am exhausted waiting, waiting for you.

Entanglement 3, 2016
From the series of 'Entanglement'
Acrylic on canvas 90 by 60 cm

Welcome to the fascinating world of entanglement. This is when two quantum particles are highly and intimately connected even when separated by huge distances in different parts of the universe! They are an inseparable whole and react as one to external forces.

A similar type of deep connectivity and correlation is shared between people and events at different points in our lives. Such connectivity makes life itself an inseparable whole.
—Ellie Lasthiotaki

22 December 2016
A Night Silver Lining
For Everyone

The Sun will come.
Enough of darkness.
Enough of wars.
We've seen the worst!

The silver lining,
I saw it coming,
I saw it in your eyes.

My Father wrote: 'My Sun',
Misspelling *son*.
I have the letter,
Just ask for it.

Sunrise is near.
The Saviour is in the skies.
Has always been
With us
Throughout the wars.

He has been here for thousands of years.
No need to look for any more messiahs.

We carry all the light,
The flame, the knowledge,
And the answer
Inside the heart!

Continued

Continuation

Just give your hand to your neighbour.
Forgive what you still can forgive.
And when you can't,
Just bring justice,
Not eye for eye.

We, people, can live forever.
We can if we only want.

We carry all the light,
The flame, the knowledge,
And the answer
Inside the heart!

We all are late to save the planet.
Its skies and oceans,
Rivers, seas . . .
We need to save all living beings.
Now that's the objective,
Let's work on that!

Then space, *κόσμος,*[*]
The universe, the stars,
The explorations,
Trips to the unknown.
Let's find what life's origin is!
Where does it all begin?

I am sure,
We all together,
We have the knowledge,

Continued

---

* From Greek, meaning 'the world'.

Continuation

We have the light,
We know the way!

We have just forgotten.
We lost the knowhow,
Le savoir faire.

I am sure,
We all together,
We have the knowledge,
We have the light,
We know the way!

Another galaxy?
Or maybe a black hole?
Let us find out.
We all need that to break the bond,
To break the curse
Of thousands of years.

We, humans, can live happily!
We can live in peace!

So why do we suffer?
Why do we create chaos, wars?
Hatred? Bombs? Disasters?

Why can't we stop?

Egypt is to be re-examined.
Some clues are still behind.

Continued

Continuation

Were the pyramids the *φάρους?*[**]
Lighthouses for the spaceships?

We need to look again
To *see* the truth,
To see *the eye*.
Perhaps, the Eye of Buddha
On a one-dollar bill.

Each detail counts.
Remember, the Devil is in the detail.
I've seen him working.
Sloppy. Makes mistakes.
Assumes he has the power.
Feels superior. Obnoxious.
To say the least.

I kept him near, as near as I only could,
To study him, his operation mode.
I learnt what I could learn.
I understood what could be understood.

What I suggest is that we play.
Is that we win his own game!

The end is near.
The end of bond with the Devil.
We paid the bill.

Continued

[**]   From Greek, accusative plural, meaning 'lighthouses'. It has been suggested to be from Ancient Greek *Φάρος* (*Pháros*, Pharos), the name of an island, on which the lighthouse of Alexandria was located, possibly from Egyptian, as well as the name of that lighthouse.

Continuation

We paid with money.
We paid in kind.
We paid with blood.
We paid enough!
He has not bought
And killed us all!

Let's come together,
United,
From around the globe.
This time for real,
This time for good.

United Nations,
Yes, we can, Obama!
We can win in an unequal fight!

In fact, we are all equal
In this unequal world:
Rich or poor,
Young or old,
As long as we can breathe the air,
As long as we can see the Sun!

Let's come together,
United,
United Nations,
Il faut monter vers les étoiles, Ariane!***

*** From French, 'One needs to go up towards the stars, Ariane!', where Ariane is a series of European civilian expendable launch vehicles for space launch use. The name comes from the French spelling of the mythological character Ariadne, who in Greek mythology was a Cretan princess. Arianespace launches Ariane rockets from the Centre Spatial Guyanais at Kourou in French Guiana, where the proximity to the equator gives a significant advantage for the launch.

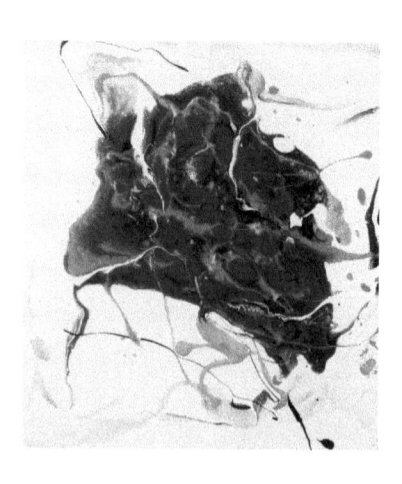

Floating, 2020
From the series of 'Life Has Many Turns'
Acrylic on wood panel 20 by 20 cm

I have always believed that one should be
prepared to expect the unexpected.
It is a paradox that emerges from what is defined as one's future.
On the one hand, one has the future that is organised or set in stone.
One is supposed to do what everyone else does: study, get a
job, love, get married, raise kids, work hard, get old . . .
On the other hand, one has *l'avenir* or the future that is unexpected,
unpredictable, unimaginable, uncontrollable, unruly . . .
One's heart pounds heavily when one crosses its path
because this future is simply irresistible.
Even if most of the time it is painful, one has a unique
chance to grow stronger and wiser out of it.

In order to perceive these unnoticeable turns in life, including
the trauma one may suffer from the inconvenience,
it is imperative that one doesn't just do what one is expected to do.
One must break the circle to identify these turns
in life. If one sleeps on the left side,
one should start sleeping on the right or change one's usual path to work . . .
These are simple, little things to prepare oneself for
the unexpected, for many turns in life.
—Ellie Lasthiotaki

4 June 2016

Subject to Interpretation
For Those Who Seek the Way

When we get trapped in clutter,
We stop to see
What *does* matter.

Change perspective.
Step aside.
Try to see from the inside.

Interpretation is the key.

The more you meditate,
The better you can see!

A Girl with Roses, 2017
Acrylic on canvas 45 by 35 cm

29 May 2016
You Are My Cup of Tea!

Kindness in words creates confidence. Kindness in thinking creates profoundness. Kindness in giving creates love.
—Lao Tzu

'The universe is so big!'
Said Father.
'Go, wander, seek!'
Said Mother.

Tonight, while stargazing
I remember
Sitting together at that table
With both Father, Mother.

I do remember
Father gave me
Next year's calendar.
Mother gave lavender
While drinking tea.

And now I clearly see:
Father gave me *time!*
Mother, on the other side,
Transmitted *flower power*
That runs in blood
On women's line!

Now, while stargazing,
I saw something truly amazing:
A shooting star,
Not even far!

Continued

Continuation

And I stopped breathing,
As I began receiving
The *power* and the *time*
From the very source of the Nile!

Establishing lost connection
Between these faint reflexions
Of the stars of the universe
And our lost world!

The energy has revived!
Let sorrow's tears subside.
We can and will be saved!

Hear the bell!
    It's *not* too late!

Human Study 1, 2016
Acrylic on paper 20 by 15 cm

29 May 2016
Oh, Baby, Hear My Questions!
The course of true love never did run smooth. —William Shakespeare

Oh, baby,

Why do you hate me,
When you need to love me?
Why do you make me suffer,
When you need to be my buffer?

Oh, baby,

Why do you pretend to me?
You know I can really feel and see
That you are not a bad guy!
So why do you do that? Why?

Oh, baby,

Why do you put on a show?
I can see things; I am not slow!
You aren't a coward!
You move fast.
Then just move forward!

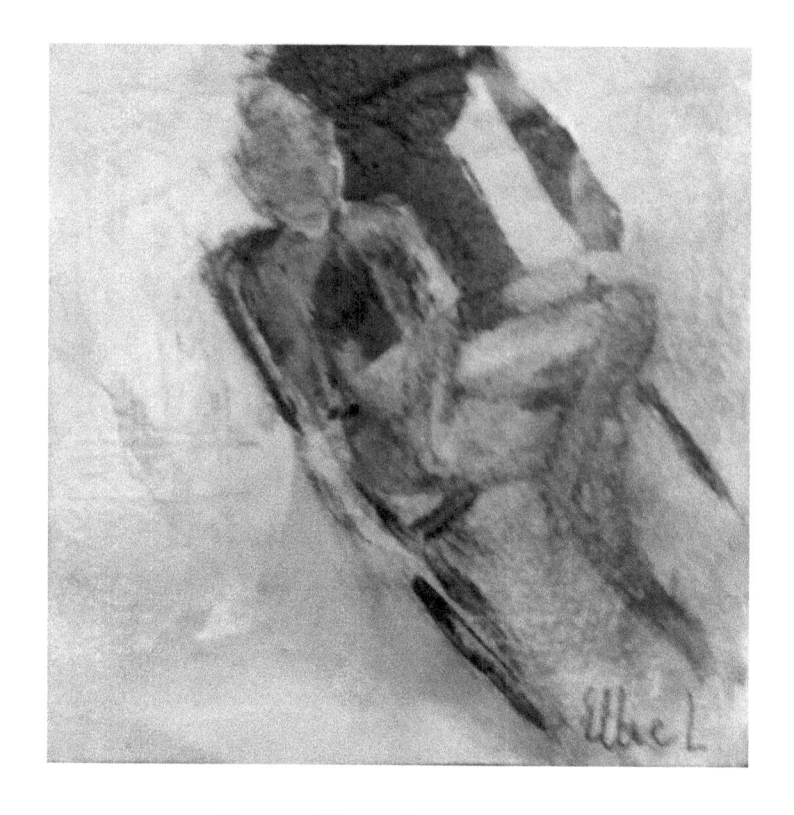

Fractured Imperfections 7, 2018
From the series of 'Fractured Imperfections'
Acrylic and gold leaf on paper 15 by 15 cm

>No matter how fractured and wounded
>a human being is, there is always light.
>All it needs is to be perceived.
>—Ellie Lasthiotaki

22 May 2016
Reunion: It Is Not Too Late!
Just for You

I don't believe that this is it,
And I shall never see you.
I think that we will meet.
We'll talk. We'll speak the truth.

What happened, happened.
Point. I am truly sorry
For everything that I've done wrong.
I suffer and I am worried.

And what I said,
Was said, when I was angry.
I am really sad.
I cannot sleep. I am not hungry.

You closed your fund.
For that as well, I am sorry!
Reunion, you love that land!
You wanted to restore its glory.

You did not fail.
It is not the end of story!
Let God prevail.
You can relaunch, don't you worry!

Just make it right.
I know you can do it.
Put up the fight.
You have all what it takes for it!

Continued

Continuation

It is *not* too late!
It is you who told me.
It is *not* too late!
My turn to tell thee.

And what do people say?
Just let them!
I tell you if I may,
Just let them!

I do not speak
Behind your back!
Believe me, I feel sad
When I hear rumours!

I am not mad!
Though I had my burden.
I tell you, I would be glad
If we could change perspectives,
If we could start it over!

It can be done.
Make a roll over!
It could be even fun!

Consider second chances!
Just make another try.
Stand through the crisis!

I am sorry if you find this long.
I had to write it.
I hope that you are strong
And you will like it.

Continued

Continuation

And to sum things up
Just know that I love you.
I do not lie. This is the fact.
It aches this much I love you!

What can I say?
That I shall wait.
And you can always call me.

Things haven't been great . . .
Think over it.
Reply or call me!

Untitled, 2019
Acrylic on wood panel 55 by 55 cm

21 May 2016
An Unanswered Invitation
Just for You

I have invited you by mail
But you have not responded.
On Friday, I asked God, I prayed
For you to feel my love, get well.
I hugged you all night long,
As long as I could hold you!

You will not come.
You have a grudge against me.
As for me, I mean no harm.
I want to hold your hand, to see thee,
To know *if we are meant to be.*

Or if I should stop to bother,
Drop it all and let you flee

Away from love, away from me,
Away forever.

Forever is a long time!
Without heart, one cannot live!
Without love, there is no life!

You will be doomed,
If you decide to flee.

You will be doomed forever.

Two Is Better Than One, 2019
Acrylic and silk screen on canvas 30 by 30 cm

19 May 2016

Adieu to He Who Does Not Exist

To say the least, this is pathetic.
Why would he lie to me?
Speak nonsense, ties magnetic
Connecting thoughts like ships at sea.

He held my icy glance,
He did not blink and lied,
Maintaining faulty stance
That there is no 'he and I'.

He had an answer, lies again,
To all the questions asked,
Yet at the end of supper, he began
To ramble and to peel off the mask.

I get it; he wants to buy some time
For him to plan to act.
And I? I want to say goodbye
And blow up this dreadful pact.

He loves me, he loves me not.
I am tired of this wicked game!
I close the book and cut the knot.
He knows, whom to blame!

Goodbye, I say adieu to you.
Go ahead and hide, and cry!
Dig yourself *dans une grotte du loup!*[*]
Deny the truth, lie, and deny!

Continued

---

[*] From French, 'in a wolf cave'.

Continuation

I am exhausted, to say the least.
Goodbye to games, to love,
To he who does not exist.

Goodbye!

Human Study 2, 2016
Acrylic on paper 20 by 15 cm

10 May 2016
One Dreadful Step Ahead
Just for You

We all have secret fears.
At night, we wipe the salt of tears.
We shake at the sight of danger
And turn the eyes away from a stranger.

What if we try at least for once
To cut the ice and fall in a mad romance?
What if we let the stranger in
And, fears aside, just look at him?

What if we let the heart beat
As wild as it would want it?
And shaking, sweating, fully red
We take that *one* dreadful step ahead?

The game is on. You play *all in*.
What can you lose by stepping in?
Your hubris, pride, and status quo,
This hanging silence . . . something more?

I doubt. Honestly, I do.
None of these things would deadly wound you.

Instead, what can you gain?
Please do not stop, do not refrain!

Open your heart, let that stranger in!
Love as much as you can breathe and feel!

A Dancing Queen, 2015
Acrylic on canvas 90 by 60 cm

30 April 2016
If I Were Your Queen!
Just for You

Was it you behind these lines?

Did you write these strokes of brush?
Letter by letter crafted by hand,
Guided by heart, led by desire?

Was it you? Did I hear your breath?

Did I feel your hands in my hair?
And your eyes on my legs?

Wait no more!
    Come from the shadows!
        Step in the light
            And love me!

And then love me some more!

Love me as if there were no tomorrow.
Let me know how you feel.

Love me as if I were your queen![*]
And I will always call you my king!

---

[*] I have always been and always will be your *Khatun*, from Mongolian, 'queen'.

Embracing the World, 2017
Acrylic on canvas 90 by 60 cm

20 April 2016
Creator's Calling
Just for You

If I could draw you,
    I would draw an early morning
    And the light shades of pink
    Dancing, floating on waves with breeze.

If I could chant you,
    I would chant a happy seagull
    With the roaring sound of the ocean
    Glad to have survived the night storm.

If I could dance you,
    I would dance a mermaid
    That did not cause the ship to wreck
    And that swam to save what could be saved.

If I could dream you,
    I would dream . . . just you,
    The way you are,
    Holding my hand, barefoot in sand.

And if I could sculpt you,
    I would sculpt the world
    As wherever you actually might be,
    You mean the world to me!

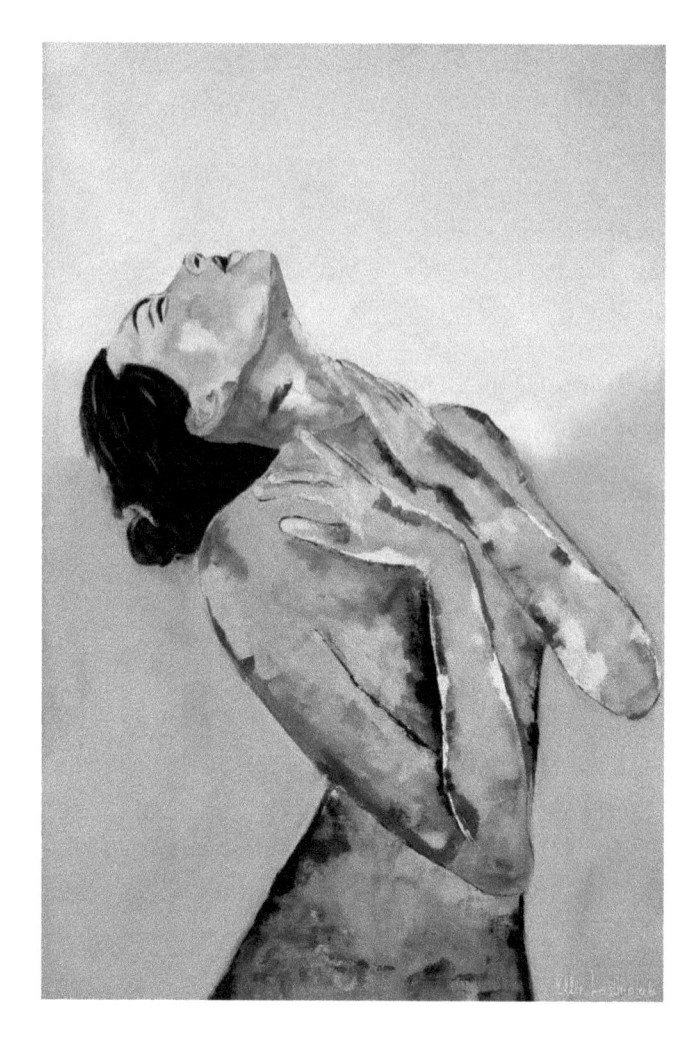

Colour the Paradise and Get In, 2018
Acrylic on canvas 90 by 60 cm

There is this moment we want to take for ourselves,
to close our eyes, to breathe in and out, to reconnect.
—Ellie Lasthiotaki

26 December 2015
Love Is Way More Durable Than Hatred
The path to paradise begins in hell. —Dante Alighieri

Over the oceans,
Under the earth,
Throughout the air,
Regardless of dirt,
I know you love me,
You adore and you cherish,
You take good care of me.

Whatever you say,
Whatever you do,
However strong you might want to seem,
When I close my eyes,
I know I did not dream,
I did not fantasise meeting you.

Maybe by fate, maybe by chance
You happened to cross my path indeed.
And you fell like a shooting star,
You fell in love with me.

You suffered a squeeze in your heart.
You tried to hide it from me.
Yet you failed, as I figured the truth,
I riddled out thee!

2005–2015 The Lost Decade

This page is left blank intentionally.[*]

---

[*] 'The Lost Decade' is lost because I did not write during this seemingly very long decade as I was unable to communicate with my Muse. It appeared that my creativity had come to a visible end. I had to be reborn from my ashes to reinvent myself and rediscover my poetic groove.

1995–2005 Discovering Love, the Essence of Life

The Choice Is Yours, 2020
Inspired by Alice Chudes' poem 'Dove's Happiness Scent'
Acrylic and charcoal on paper 30 by 20 cm

4 Janvier 2002

*Deux Colombes,
l'Âme de l'Océan*

Juste pour Toi

Je n'ai jamais été
Si heureuse
Que maintenant.
Je n'ai jamais respiré
Si profondément
Que ce mois-ci.

Je n'ai jamais senti
Cette odeur
Du bonheur
Qui se répand
Le matin
Et qui reste
Jusqu'au soir.

Je n'ai jamais voyagé
Avec mon amour
Dans le sable
De la mer,
Dans les nuages
Des dunes.

Tout oublié
Et tout derrière,
On dansait
Parmi les bateaux
Sur une île cachée.

Continued

---

4 January 2002

*Dove's
Happiness Scent*

Just for You

I've never been
This happy before.
I've never breathed
This unreservedly.

I've never felt
This happiness scent
That embraces you
From dawn till dusk.

I've never travelled
With the love of my life,
Following in God's footsteps
In the sand of the sea,
Bathing in the clouds of the dunes.

Having forgotten everything,
Having left all troubles behind,
We were dancing
Among the ships
On an island
Lost in the immensity of the ocean.

We were just like
Two doves,
Free and joyful.
We were the soul of this world.

Continuation

On était	Having forgotten
Deux colombes,	Everything,
L'âme de l'océan,	Having endless
Tout oublié	Opportunities
Et tout devant.	In front of us.

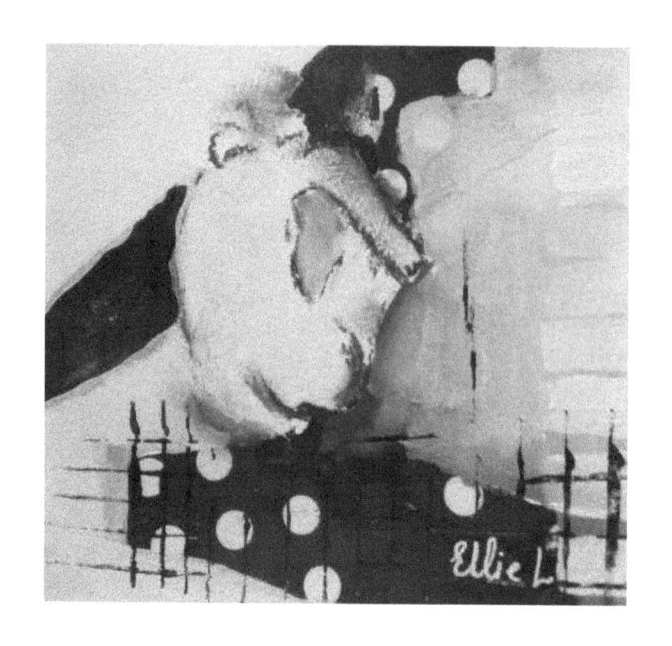

Fractured Imperfections 12, 2018
From the series of 'Fractured Imperfections'
Acrylic and gold leaf on paper 15 by 15 cm
In private collection

> No matter how fractured and wounded
> a human being is, there is always light.
> All it needs is to be perceived.
> —Ellie Lasthiotaki

31 Juillet 2001
Mon Cœur Rayonne
Juste pour Toi

Écoute mon cœur :
Il bat pour toi !
Il bat pour toi tout seul !
Tu es le monde entier pour moi !
Tu es ma foi et mon bonheur !

Je t'aime, chéri, de tout mon cœur,
De toutes les forces que j'ai.
Je t'aime comme je n'ai aimé…
        Personne!
Et comme personne n'a su m'aimer.

Tu viens le soir et je t'embrasse,
J'y pense après toute la journée.
Je te regarde, je retiens tes phrases
Et je te rappelle que tu es très aimé !

Écoute mon cœur :
Il bat pour toi !
Il bat pour toi tout seul !
Tu es le monde entier pour moi !
Tu es ma foi et mon bonheur !

Écoute mon cœur :
Mon cœur rayonne !
Et il rayonne pour toi !

31 July 2001
A Beam from My Heart
Just for You

Listen to my heart:
It beats for you!
And only for you, my dear!
You mean the world to me!
You are my faith, my desire!

I love you, my precious,
With all of my heart,
As strongly as I only can.
I love you as I have never loved anyone.
And as no one has ever loved me.

You come in the evening,
I hug you; I kiss you.
I think about that all day long
The following day.

I like to look at you, my darling.
I try to memorise all that you convey.
And I remind you,
Hear me say,
That my love for you is everlasting!

Listen to my heart:
It beats for you!
And only for you, my dear!
You mean the world to me!
You are my faith, my desire!

That's what my heart
In silence beams to yours.

The Hidden Urban Marvel, 2019
Acrylic on canvas 90 by 90 cm
In private collection

26 Janvier 2001
*La Fève de la
Galette des Rois*
Juste pour Toi

Écoute, chéri, je veux te dire
Que la vie est merveilleuse.
Mon bonheur,
C'est toi,
Et ça veut dire
Que tu me rends heureuse.

Et aujourd'hui tu m'as offert
Des roses sublimes toutes rouges.
Et moi, je veux t'offrir ces vers
En t'embrassant
De bouche à bouche.

Tu es mon prince, mon fiancé
Qui es venu de mes rêves.
Et toute ma vie je vais t'aimer,
Mon roi
Dont j'ai trouvé la fève !

Je pense à toi et me réjouis.
Je t'imagine plus tard
Avec des gamins à toi et moi
Qui courent
En se marrant.

Écoute, chéri, je veux te dire
Que la vie est merveilleuse.
Mon bonheur,
C'est toi,
Et ça veut dire
Que tu me rends heureuse.

26 January 2001
*Twelfth Night
Cake's Charm*
Just for You

Listen to me, my dear,
I want to tell you
That our life is just marvellous.
My well-being is embodied by you.
And that means
That you make me really happy.

Today you offered me
A gorgeous bouquet of red roses.
And I wish to gift these verses to you
In my turn,
Kissing you vigorously
Time and time again.

You are my fiancé, my prince,
Who descended straight from my dreams.
I will love you for all my life,
My king, whose charm
I found hidden in a Twelfth Night cake!

I think of you and I rejoice.
I imagine you many years later
With kids, both yours and mine,
Running around, laughing.

Listen to me, my dear,
I want to tell you
That our life is just marvellous.
My well-being is embodied by you.
And that means
That you make me really happy.

Fractured Imperfections 8, 2018
From the series of 'Fractured Imperfections'
Acrylic and gold leaf on paper 15 by 15 cm
In private collection

No matter how fractured and wounded
a human being is, there is always light.
All it needs is to be perceived.
—Ellie Lasthiotaki

9 Décembre 2000
Tu Es Mon Étoile Filante
Juste pour Toi

Depuis toujours
Je te cherchais
Et puis un jour
Je t'ai trouvé
Sur la planète
Où nous vivions.

J'ai vu tes yeux
Et j'ai compris
Qu'il ne fallait pas partir.
Tu m'as vaincu par ton sourire
Et par ton charme
Que j'ai senti.

Je suis si bien
Quand tu me rassures !
Quand tu me prends dans tes bras !
Je suis si bien jour après jour !
Je suis si bien
Quand tu es là !

Et même si la vie n'est pas facile,
Nous la rendrons jolie !
Nous surpasserons tous les soucis
Et nous ferons de la magie !

Tout ce que j'ai dit,
Tout cela est vrai,
Il faut y croire, c'est tout !

Je viens de voir une étoile filante.
Tu y crois ? –
Pourtant je l'ai bien vue !

9 December 2000
You Are My Shooting Star
Just for You

I have been looking for you since forever.
And then one day
I found my Earthly heaven
Right here, among the living,
Because I encountered you.

I saw your eyes
And realised
I couldn't let you go!

You won me over
With your smile.
And with your charm
You conquered my fears.

I feel so good, when you reassure me!
When you embrace me kindly!
I feel so good time and time again!
I feel so good, when you are here for me!

Even if life can be hard sometimes,
Together we will make it awesome!
We will transcend all of life's hurdles
And we will make it simply miraculous!

All the above,
All that is true.
Just believe,
Just believe in it!

Did you see a shooting star?
Well, I did.
So, should you!

The Tree of Happiness, 2016
Acrylic on canvas 90 by 60 cm

5 Novembre 2000

*L'Aspiration d'une
Petite Fille*

Juste pour Toi

I. Une Vision du Futur

Il y a longtemps,
J'étais petite
Et je rêvais chaque nuit
D'un prince charmant,
Quelqu'un de solide,
Avec lequel je fuirais
Dans une forêt
Pleine de mystères
Sur un cheval magique
Voir les étoiles de la soirée
Tout près de la mer…
Et n'être plus petite !

II. Un Vœux Qui Se Réalise

Et aujourd'hui,
Le jour venu,
Mon prince charmant
Est dans ma vie.
Je ne rêve plus
Mais je l'entends
Tout près de moi
À me parler.
Je sens ses mains
Et je crois

Continued

5 November 2000

*The Yearning of
a Little Girl*

Just for You

I. A Projection into the Future

I remember myself
As a little girl.
I lie in bed daydreaming
And I yearn.

I yearn for a prince charming,
My soulmate, flesh and blood.
I dream he is coming
To make me happy, not sad.

I see us together,
As he kisses me tenderly.
We are in love forever,
Managed to escape the reality.

There, in a mystic forest
On a vigorous white horse
We become the finest,
The best versions of ourselves.

Near sea, we stargaze.
Lost on purpose,
So, no one can find us!
I smile, truly amazed.
I am a princess and no longer a child!

Continuation

Que c'est un Vrai Amour !
Je touche ses doigts,
Je regarde ses yeux
Et je lui dis bonjour.

III. L'Aventure Qui Est Devant

Il est heureux,
Je suis heureuse.
On a quitté la terre
Sur un bateau,
Dans une rivière
Qui porte bonheur
De finesse de verre.

Cheveux au vent,
Les yeux ouverts,
C'est l'aventure
Qui est devant.
C'est le soleil qui a ouvert
Tous les chemins de demain !

II. A Dream Come True

Today, I cannot be happier.
As today is *the day*
I met my prince charming!
All my fears, all my struggles
Are finally left at bay!

I am no longer dreaming.
Rather, I hear him speak.
I stand very near,
Leaning on him,
As the clock ticks.

The rain outside pours.
He holds me very tight.
And I just know that
He is my love, my fairy knight.

III. An Adventure Together

He is joyous. I am even more so.
We left the shore behind
On a boat in a deep rapid river,
Our happiness to be able to hide.

I let the breeze comb my hair.
His eyes are wide shut.
An adventure together is rare.
Our anchor is already tied
With a knot.

Wherever the river flows,
Wherever the boat takes us,
The Sun always knows
How to light our path.

All It Takes Is a Flower, 2018
Acrylic on paper 20 by 15 cm

14 July 2000

A Thought of Gratitude
For Larry

Starry, starry night.

I cannot express
How thankful am I
To those who came to help.

Starry, starry night.

I am thinking
Of all the good things
That you've done,
That you've done for us.

Starry, starry night.

I know time may fly,
Fly away as birds can do,
But the dolphins will still play,
As I think of you!

Freedom Is Bravery, 2017
Acrylic on canvas 150 by 100 cm

τό δ' εὔδαιμον τό ἐλεύθερον, τὸ δ'ἐλεύθερον τό εὔψυχον

Freedom makes a man happy, and freedom is the bravery of the heart.
—Pericles' Funeral Oration, Thucydides History of the Peloponnesian War, 431–404 BC (2.43.4)

My life and my art are inspired by this quote. Perhaps, because of my Greek name given at birth, Eleftheria. It has always defined me in my choices in life. I always knew it was more than a name. It was an introduction to intellectual freedom, the freedom to choose, to experiment in life, to express myself without fear.
—Ellie Lasthiotaki

20 Mai 2000
La Soif de Liberté
Juste pour Toi

Plus haut ! Plus loin !

De ce monde de réalistes !

Plus haut ! Plus loin !

Pour tracer de nouvelles pistes !

Vers le ciel et les étoiles,
Vers ce monde idéal
Qui se cache derrière la lune.
Trouve de l'eau derrière la dune !

Plus haut ! Plus loin !

La liberté n'est gagnée
Que par un cœur courageux !

Plus haut ! Plus loin !

La liberté n'est donnée
Que pour te rendre heureux !

20 May 2000
Thirst for Freedom
Just for You

Fly higher! Fly away!

Detach yourself from
This materialistic world!
Find a way to reach new horizons!

Fly towards your wildest dreams!

Fly higher! Fly away!

Fly towards the skies!

Fly towards the stars!

Find a trace of another dimension!
It is concealed in
The shadow of the Moon
Like an oasis in the desert!

Fly higher! Fly away!

Fly towards your wildest dreams!

Fly higher! Fly away!

Do the impossible!
Fight for your freedom
Inside your brave heart!
It will render you happy!

Dreamy Sunset, 2020
Acrylic on canvas 90 by 90 cm

1 Septembre 1999
*Une Heureuse Pensée
à Propos de la Vie*

Il y a des moments où l'on est heureux simplement parce qu'on vit, parce qu'on respire, parce qu'on est dans ce monde.

Le soleil brille et cela apporte le bonheur éternel. Le bonheur qu'il faut apprécier et savoir garder dans son âme pour toujours.

C'est ce qu'on appelle *la vie*.

---

1 September 1999
*A Happy Thought
About Life*

There are moments when one is happy simply because one lives, because one breathes, because one is in this world.

The Sun is shining, and this brings eternal happiness inside one's heart. Such happiness one needs to be able to appreciate and know how to keep in one's soul forever.

That's what it means *to have a life*.

Fractured Imperfections 9, 2018
From the series of 'Fractured Imperfections'
Acrylic and gold leaf on paper 15 by 15 cm
In private collection

> No matter how fractured and wounded
> a human being is, there is always light.
> All it needs is to be perceived.
> —Ellie Lasthiotaki

20 Août 1999
La Brume de Demain
Juste pour Toi

L'avenir est caché
Dans la brume de demain.

La moindre chose peut en changer
Pour toujours le destin.

Demain est ouvert
À tous les changements
Mais quand même,
On choisit
Sans hésiter
Juste *un* des *chemins* !

On n'est pas sûr d'abord
Si c'est ce qu'il nous faut.
On regrette, on s'en doute.
On y passe
Des heures et des heures.

Mais quand on se tourne
Pour voir le passé,
On s'aperçoit d'un coup
Que s'était cela
Ce qu'on cherchait !

Ça nous arrive un jour
Mais le jour suivant

L'avenir est toujours
Caché
Dans la brume de demain.

---

20 August 1999
The Mist of Destiny
Just for You

Fate is disguised
In the mist of tomorrow.

What will it be: Hell? Paradise?
Great joy or deep sorrow?

Next day encompasses
Countless chances.
Yet as time passes,
You realise you travel along
Only one of *the forking paths!*

At first, you are not sure.
Are you on *the right way?*
You get tempted, get lured
To wander, to stray away.

Nonetheless, you continue
To walk in the steps
Of *your chosen path*.
Will you reach destination?
    Your venue?
Or will you, discouraged,
    Turn back?

Every day brings about a choice.
You select where you actually are.

Yet the next day, fate is still veiled,
Because in the mist
You can't see far!

Meditating, 2017
Acrylic on canvas 90 by 60 cm

20 Août 1999
Le Courant de la Vie
Pour Natka

L'avenir vient en courant.
On le ralentit
Un peu parfois.
Sinon, on plonge dans le courant
Qui nous emmène
Vite, pas lentement,
Dans un endroit
Où l'on se sent bien,
Où le temps
N'est qu'une illusion qui vient,
Qui vient et qui va,
Comme le vent au printemps.

20 August 1999
The Current of Life
For Natka

Time is like *a current of air*,
Whose sudden gusts
Our future bring.

Time is like *a current of water*,
Osmosis of temporal matter,
Which wells up faster in spring.

Our future rushes upon us.
We attempt to slow it down,
As we swim in the current
That is too fast!

This stream brings us around
To where we should actually be.
So we shouldn't battle,
We need to just let it be!

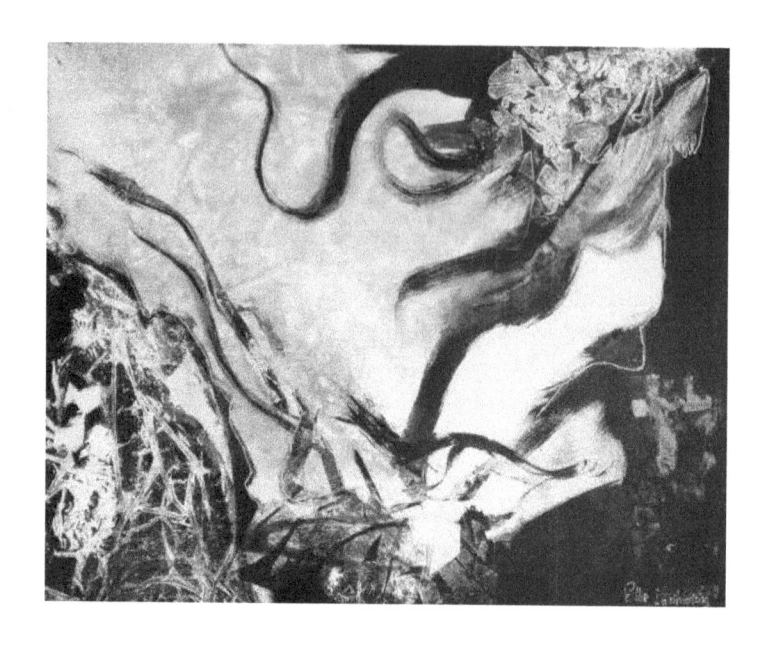

Feel and Liber, 2019
Mixed media on canvas 90 by 60 cm

> I am multidimensional. I have always taken risks.
> So, even if everything goes wrong, at least I feel alive pursuing it.
> —Ellie Lasthiotaki

1 May 1999
A Restless Traveller
For Eli, Irwin, Nirav, Ohad, and Paul
Twenty years from now, you will be more disappointed by the things you didn't do than by the ones you did do. So, throw off the bowlines. Sail away from the safe harbour. Catch the trade winds in your sails. Explore. Dream. Discover.
—Mark Twain

Who am I?

> A traveller who walks far,
> Only despairing mist around.

What do I seek for on this strange path?

> Perhaps, a Motherland where I belong,
> A fairy realm, where good wins over evil,
> And life is a joy!

Where is that land?

> I fear I can never find it.

Who am I?

> A traveller resigned to walk far.

Don't Cry, 2015
Acrylic on paper 30 by 25 cm

1 April 1999

A Motherly Gaze
For My Mother

My mom, my dear mom,
I saw a dream,
I saw your eyes

That looked in sadness
Into my eyes.

I felt a gentle pain
That squeezed my heart,
And lonely loving light
Embraced the night.

My dear mom,
I heard your voice,
I saw your eyes.

Echoes of Spring, 2015
Acrylic on canvas 90 by 60 cm
In private collection

8 March 1999

Dancing Snow
Just for You

Snow under the light
Dances in a dream.
Sweeps away my mind
Catching fairy theme.

Snow whitens dark
Making joy to live;
Wonders in the sky
I have never seen.

Wind embraces thee,
Snow cools my face.
What a pretty night!
What a lovely space!

Snow under the light.
Echoes of spring.
Sweeps away my mind,
As I dance and sing.

The Golden Paths, 2015
Acrylic and gold leaf on canvas 40 by 30 cm

27 February 1999

A Rhetorical Question for Motherland

He who has overcome his fears will truly be free. —Aristotle

Russia, *Mother Russia*,
Where are you going,
    Suffering along a hard road?

Will you walk blindly through fire and flames?
    Or will you be able to avoid the troubles,
    Avoid the extremes?
    And yet, *will you persevere?*

What is ahead?

Only uncertainty:
One cannot predict your future.

Mysteriously, as people say,
Though you pursue the hardest path,
You overcome with a proud beauty
    Terrors and wars,
    Fear and death.

Over the centuries, the exquisite Russian beauty
And the generous Russian spirit
Have penetrated the hearts of countless people
Around the world.

Regardless, no one can understand
    The depths of a Russian Soul.

How is that you remain so strong?
    So beautiful, so majestic?

Continued

Continuation

Yet is it also true that you are destined
    To be in darkness, mud, and cold forever?
And everything that one can find in Russian people—
    Talent, beauty, an inherent goodness—
Will be shaded by *laissez-faire*? Stupidity?
    Arrogance? Dishonesty? Slothfulness?

Is it possible that one day you could be
    A country where one is free to breathe?

Russia, *Mother Russia*,
Where are you going,
    Suffering along a hard road?

Could you be a gentler mother?
    Could you rise at last from your knees?

The Desire, 2018
From the series of 'Life Has Many Turns'
Acrylic on wood panel 100 by 100 cm

I have always believed that one should be
prepared to expect the unexpected.
It is a paradox that emerges from what is defined as one's future.
On the one hand, one has the future that is organised or set in stone.
One is supposed to do what everyone else does: study, get a
job, love, get married, raise kids, work hard, get old . . .
On the other hand, one has *l'avenir* or the future that is unexpected,
unpredictable, unimaginable, uncontrollable, unruly . . .
One's heart pounds heavily when one crosses its path
because this future is simply irresistible.
Even if most of the time it is painful, one has a unique
chance to grow stronger and wiser out of it.

In order to perceive these unnoticeable turns in life, including
the trauma one may suffer from the inconvenience,
it is imperative that one doesn't just do what one is expected to do.
One must break the circle to identify these turns
in life. If one sleeps on the left side,
one should start sleeping on the right or change one's usual path to work . . .
These are simple, little things to prepare oneself for
the unexpected, for many turns in life.
—Ellie Lasthiotaki

24 Janvier 1999

Enlevée par le Vent

Mis en musique par Robert Agis dans la 'Chanson d'Amour de Cyrano de Bergerac'
© 2000 par Robert Agis*

Lui :
Quand je rêve, je vois
    Ton beau visage ;
Je t'imagine souriante
    Sur cette plage ;
Mais quand je me réveille,
    Le sable est froid,
Car tu n'es plus là-bas.

Je suis seul, seul sans toi ;
Tu es loin, mais pourquoi ?
Je suis seul, seul j'y suis,
Égaré, malbâti.

Elle :
À travers l'océan, je t'écris :
Excuse-moi, je t'en supplie !
C'est le vent
    Qui m'a prise
Et les vagues élevées
    Par la brise.

Continued

---

24 January 1999

The Other Side of the Mirror

Set to music by Robert Agis in the song 'Chanson d'Amour de Cyrano de Bergerac'
© 2000 by Robert Agis*

He:
When I dream, I see
    Your beautiful face.
I imagine you standing
    On this beach
But when I wake up
    In this cold sand,
There is no longer a trace,
    No sign of you in this land.

I am alone without you, on my own.
You are gone. I scream: Why?
I am alone here, all alone!
Lost, not feeling myself, I cry.

She:
I write to you from a lost sphere:
Forgive me, I am held in fee!
I am trapped on the other side
    Of the mirror
In another dimension
    You cannot see.

---

* The poem 'Enlevée par le Vent' appears as the lyrics to the song 'Chanson d'Amour de Cyrano de Bergerac'.
Words © 2000 by Yelena Zemtsova and Robert Agis.
Music © 2000 by Robert Agis.
All rights reserved.

Continuation

Je suis seule, délaissée,
Seule sans toi, isolée,
Je ne vois que la noirceur,
La douleur dans mon cœur.

Lui :
Je suis seul, seul sans toi ;
Tu es loin, mais pourquoi ?
Je suis seul, seul j'y suis,
Égaré, malbâti.

I feel abandoned, alone,
Far away from you.
I can't repay what I owe.
What is broken I cannot glue.

My heart suffers in silence.
Darkness covered my thoughts.
I can't explain
    This separation violence.
I can't get away
    Not being caught.

He:
I am alone without you, on my own.
You are gone. I scream: Why?
I am alone here, all alone!
Lost, not feeling myself, I cry.

Fractured Imperfections 10, 2018
From the series of 'Fractured Imperfections'
Acrylic and gold leaf on paper 15 by 15 cm
In private collection

> No matter how fractured and wounded
> a human being is, there is always light.
> All it needs is to be perceived.
> —Ellie Lasthiotaki

9 Janvier 1999
Une Lettre d'Amour
Juste pour Toi

Mon cher,
Je t'écris
Une lettre d'amour.
Écoute, je t'en supplie :
Je t'aime pour toujours !

Je t'aime dans l'aurore
Quand le soleil se lève.
Je t'aime jusqu'à la mort
Quand la nuit t'enlève.

Je t'aime dans l'océan
De mes rêves, de mes larmes.
Mon amour, mon miracle ancien,
Tu me protèges par tes armes.

Mon soleil et ma lune,
Mes étoiles sur le ciel,
Je t'écris, mon air pur :
Je pense à toi sans arrêt !

---

9 January 1999
A Love Letter
Just for You

My dear,
Here is my love letter for you.
Believe me as it's really true:
'I will always care,
Will always love you!'

I will love you at dawn,
When the Sun shows its first ray.
And I will love you,
Till the darkness steals you away.

My love is like an endless ocean,
Ocean of tears, ocean of dreams.
You are my ancient love potion,
My miracle that in silence beams.

You are my Sun and my Moon,
My stars in the sky.
I am writing to you:
'I need you to breathe, else I die!'

The Bridge of Hope, 2016
Acrylic on canvas 90 by 60 cm

9 January 1999
The Music of My Heart
Just for You

My love, may I share
My insights with you?
I love you. I care.
I will write all my stories for you!

You are the music,
The tune, which lightens my heart.
You give me the fluids
To dance the ballet of life.

You bring me a song
With lyrics illuminating my path.
You make what is wrong
To flee
In the Sun of the right.

You are the music,
The tune, which lightens my heart.
You give me the fluids
To dance the ballet of life.

You build a miracle bridge
Of hope and love
Over the mountain ridge
Far away, far above.

You are the music,
The tune, which lightens my heart.
You give me the fluids
To dance the ballet of life.

Continued

Continuation

You broaden my horizons.
You open my eyes.
You are what I've searched for,
My precious, my soul, my life.

Through Your Eyes I Could Dream the Sky, 2019
Acrylic on canvas 40 by 40 cm

Inspired by the natural world, the fight for their lives,
the crossing of rivers but also the maternal love,
I burst into tears watching a baby zebra trying
to cross a river with crocodiles.
Its mother lost it and had to return, risking her own life.
Eventually they found each other.
—Ellie Lasthiotaki

24 Novembre 1998
Un Rêve de Midi
Pour Avi

La vie est une lithographie
    Sans couleurs.
Nous ne voyons que le noir,
    Que les soucis.
Nous oublions
    Le bonheur.

Mon enfance a passé assez vite.
Je m'en rappelle plus ou moins :
C'est le soleil qui me sourit,
C'est la pluie que j'entends de loin.

Tout à coup,
    J'ai commencé à grandir.
Ce qui veut dire que
    Je n'étais plus là.
J'attendais que
    Le monde se mette à ouvrir
Toutes ses merveilles
    En ne refusant rien.

Et puis j'ai rêvé qu'un jour
Je comprenne *le secret de la vie* :
Ce pourquoi j'ai vu le jour,
Ce pourquoi je vis.

24 November 1998
A Midday Dream
For Avi

Life is a zebra
    In black and white.
We remember the trauma.
We tend to forget
    The bright side.

My childhood ended abruptly.
I remember some, some I forgot.
I recall the Sun that smiles to me.
I recall the rain that cries a lot.

Suddenly,
    I was an adult grown up.
My native town
    Wasn't any longer big enough.
I was longing for more,
    For the world to open up,
To uncover its wonders,
    To take secrets apart.

And I dreamt that one day
I would understand
The secret of life:
Why it is that I live,
That I am alive.

Take a Breath In, 2018
Acrylic on canvas 90 by 60 cm

There is this moment we want to take for ourselves,
to close our eyes, to breathe in and out, to reconnect.
—Ellie Lasthiotaki

24 Novembre 1998
Tombée Amoureuse
Juste pour Toi

Quelquefois
    Pendant ma vie,
La lumière
    Ensoleillait la nuit !

Et la pluie ne pleurait plus ;
Et les fleurs me faisaient la rue.

C'est l'amour,
    C'est le bonheur !
C'est une chanson somptueuse
    Pour le cœur.

Mon roi des rêves
    Venu du ciel
Qui me répète
    Que je suis belle !

---

24 November 1998
Fallen in Love
Just for You

I am in love. In love I am!
Darkness is faded away by the Sun!

My mind floats, capricious.
Even rain feels auspicious.

My heart races in a flower field.
I daydream, head in a right tilt.

Love for me is a pure joy!
A tune in my heart.
    My favourite toy.

A song from my prince
    From the skies
Who is telling me
    Such beautiful lies!

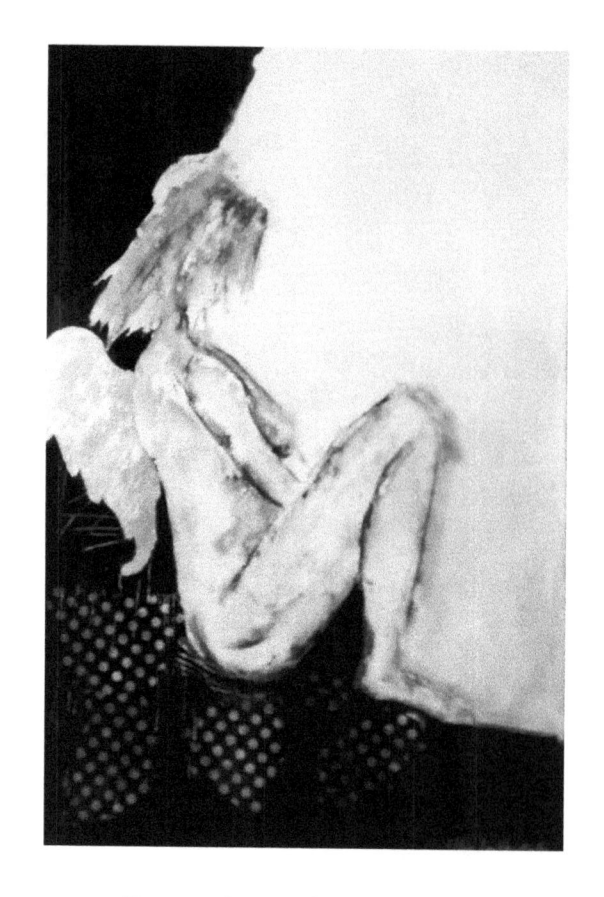

Fractured Imperfections 1, 2018
From the series of 'Fractured Imperfections'
Acrylic and gold leaf on paper 15 by 15 cm
In private collection

> No matter how fractured and wounded
> a human being is, there is always light.
> All it needs is to be perceived.
> —Ellie Lasthiotaki

24 Novembre 1998
À l'Amie du Cœur
Pour Sacha

Je t'écris en souriant :
'Où es-tu, que fais-tu là-bas ?'

Je t'ai promis que je viendrais
Pour qu'on puisse partager

Toutes les pensées
    Et toutes les erreurs,
Tout ce qu'il nous arrive
    Chaque heure,

Tout ce qui est dit dans le vent
    Qui est immortel pourtant.

24 November 1998
To My Dear Friend
For Sasha

I am smiling to you:
'What are you up to?
    Where are you?'

Promises kept, I am here with you.
Here to share between us two

All our thoughts,
    All the mistakes,
Everything that has happened to us,

All that is gone away with the wind,
Gone but lives immortal within.

My Little Ballerina, 2016
Acrylic on paper 40 by 30 cm

10 Novembre 1998
Une Lettre à Ma Fille

Ne sois pas aussi sensible
Comme ta mère l'était toujours.
C'est pour toi que c'est pénible,
Chaque instant de tous les jours.

Je te dis que dans ce monde
Il n'y a pas de justice.
Ne la cherche pas,
    Je te le demande,
Ne la désire pas,
    Je t'en prie !

Moi aussi,
    J'ai fait des fautes !
    Je ne suis pas un idéal.

Ton chemin,
    Qu'il soit meilleur
    Que le mien
    Et plus global !

10 November 1998
A Letter to My Daughter

Darling, don't be as sensitive
As your mom has always been.
It would make your life
    So distressing
Every moment
    That you live each day.

Now, I wish also to tell you
That there is no justice
    In this world.
Please, do not look for it,
Do not even long for it either!

I too was mistaken
    Time and time again!
I am far from being perfect,
    Can you see?
I wish that you'd have a better plan,
A better life:
As good as a life can be!

Who Am I? 2019
Acrylic on paper 20 by 20 cm

27 June 1998
The Hidden Sense of Life
A Note for Myself

Seek new things.
Find them.
Seek again.
Explore.
And never stop this process.

This is the hidden sense of life.
I think so.
Or no, I am sure!

Fire and Ice, 2018
Acrylic on paper 35 by 25 cm

26 Janvier 1998
Une Vague Idée de l'Amour
Juste pour Toi

Je n'ai qu'une vague idée,
    Une idée de toi,
Et pourtant dans le monde entier
    C'est ce qui est
    Le plus important pour moi.

Je ne rêve de personne
    Sauf toi,
    Mon amour,
        Mon meilleur ami.

Je ne cherche que toi,
Je n'ai pas d'autres envies.

Je n'ai pas d'autre but
    Que t'aimer
        Pour moi !

---

26 January 1998
A Faint Image of Love
Just for You

I have only a faint image
Of who you really might be.
Yet that's for me in the world
The most significant key.

It is you whom I dream about,
Day or night,
Asleep or awake,
Only you, my love,
Only you, my best friend.

This is my only desire,
I wish to find you.

I do not see any other,
Any other life's purpose
    Than to love you!

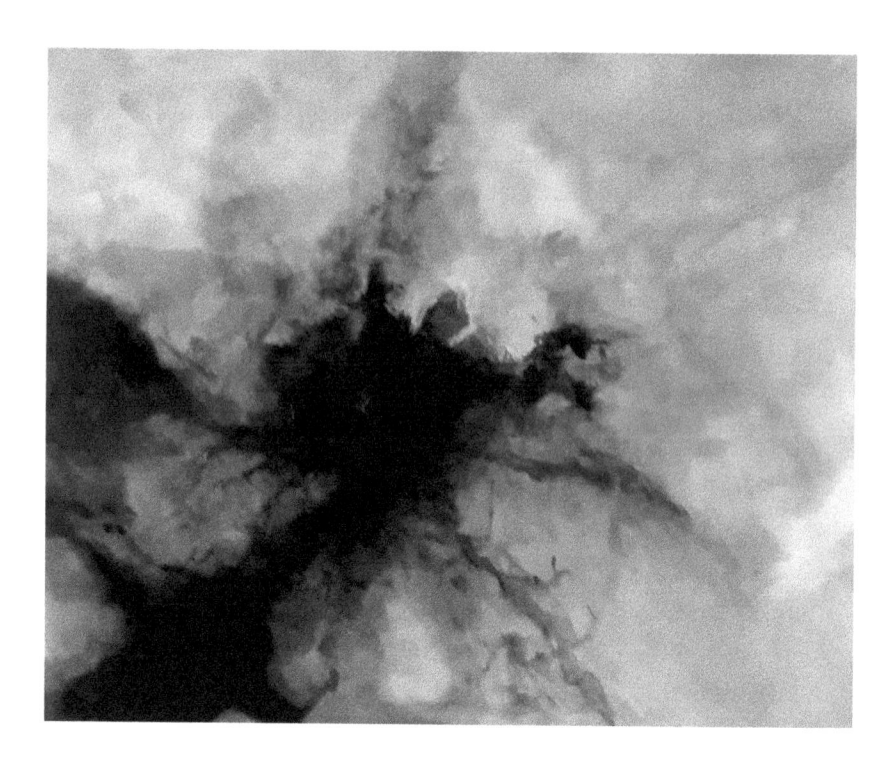

The Promise of the Unexpected Light, 2018
Finalist at The International Artist Grand Prize Competition 2019, Taiwan
Acrylic on canvas 90 by 60 cm

Secret, parallel lives, worlds here and there, places we lived, memories, reminiscent voices of people we met, loved, dear voices… Then we lose them, but the sound of their music has left a trace in our minds, thoughts, subconscious.
—Ellie Lasthiotaki

11 Octobre 1997
La Lumière Divine
Juste pour Toi

Je voudrais remplacer le désespoir
    Et les ténèbres
Par des lueurs d'espoir
    Et de la lumière :
La Lumière Divine,
    L'espoir pour tous.

Et puis je l'aime.
Oui, je l'aime
Parce qu'il est le soleil
Et la lumière pour moi.

11 October 1997
The Divine Light
Just for You

I would like to replace
    Darkness and despair
    With light and hope:
The Divine Light,
    Hope for everyone.

And then I love him.
    Yes, I love him,
Because he is like
The sunlight
    For me.

The Linear Path, 2015
Acrylic on canvas 90 by 60 cm
In private collection

People live parallel lives in analogous realities. Their lives deviate here and there, but no matter their race, status, or origin, people are all the same everywhere.
—Ellie Lasthiotaki

5 March 1997
Will the World Ever Change?
For Tsafi

I love people so much,
    And I'd like people to love me.

I admire the world I live in,
    And I'd like it to be kind to me.

I know it is not good enough,
    But it is people who make it unpleasant and bad.

I'm well aware my efforts will fall,
    I won't make the world to stop being wrong.

But nonetheless, I hope it'll change.
    Maybe in time it will be less strange.
    Maybe in time people will stop seeking revenge.

    It will be then when the world will change!

Detail, Seize the Day in Blues, 2020
Acrylic on wood panel 120 by 60 cm
In private collection

23 November 1996
A Play on Words

'I was up but I was down,'
Said a funny little clown.
Being out and about,
He is back instead of being out.

Then he turned his head ahead
And 'Light is on!' he said.
'Wow' was abroad in the crowd.
'Look at it and think about!'

Otherworldly Perception, 2019
Acrylic on canvas 100 by 100 cm

Afterword

My Musings about Life

> Beauty awakens the soul to act.
> —Dante Alighieri

In Russian, svet, *свет*, means both the light and the world. While the *white light*, *белый свет*, means this world, the world of the living, *that light*, *тот свет*, means the next world, the world of the dead. It literally describes the world of the afterlife as a distinct kind of the light. I came back to life from a near-death experience and thus can testify myself how different that light was from anything that I have seen in this world: the light of the Sun, the light of a candle, the light of an electric bulb, the light of a campfire, the light of a computer screen . . .

Among paintings in my art collection, there are two in particular that I would like to speak about. Their title is *Dve storony sveta*, *Две стороны света*. At first, I translated it as 'Two Sides of the Light', however, after some brainstorming, rather as 'Two Parallel Worlds'.

The first of the two lithographs depicts a young girl, maybe eight or nine years old, facing an older man, maybe her father, maybe her grandfather, maybe someone she knows, who looks above her head. She is eager to talk with him, but what he has to say to her is literally *above her,* as she is just too young to understand him. This artwork together with the memory of my grandfather teaching me the rudiments of poetry in 1988 inspired my poem 'A Seed of Knowledge'.

The second lithograph is more complex. One sees a young beautiful woman looking in the emptiness in front of her. She is drawn on a white background, as if to say that she is among the living. The other half of the image is filled with black shadows of several old men. They are shouting something to her, maybe a warning, but she does not hear them. Their interaction is undermined by the invisible division between the two parallel worlds that never cross, yet the young woman *feels* that they are trying to communicate with her, as she is looking in the right direction. Can she ever decipher their message? And if not her, who might be capable to do that in her stead? Did these ghosts pick her to speak to precisely because *she stood a chance* to succeed at interpreting the subtle message from beyond? Or maybe because her subconscious was attuned to the forces of nature?

As I look at this lithograph, I see the young girl from the first painting that grew up. All her forefathers passed away. It is they who try to connect with her in a desperate attempt. They communicate through her premonitions, visions, dreams, intuitions, sixth sense, *déjà vu*, even her DNA. All these are intangible bridges to other realities that I use in my poetry, which should be read not only in the first degree but rather multidimensionally.

Dreams happen when we unlock our unconscious mind, when we let go of this reality. Premonitions are another kind of dreaming. They happen, when we are awake, but when we let our subconscious speak. Next to that is the state of trance, when we momentarily leave our body and connect with our soul. Near-death experiences are yet another form of sensing the paranormal.

My saga of nearly twenty-five years in duration is about searching for answers, rigorous self-examination, personal evolution. I try to dissect the meaning of life, if life has a meaning!

What if each and every one of us had a mission that one needs to accomplish? Most of us fail as we live without thinking, without realising, what exactly we are doing in this world. And we die only to be reborn again with the same mission but having forgotten about our previous life. So we are given another *try*. Yet we fail time and time again. We fail each and every time of our existence, when we did not care to connect with our soul, when we did not manage *to see the light*.

This is how I perceive it today: the eternal fight within myself whether to walk the road of my fate.

I may choose not to comply, or I may choose to follow God's plan for me. Thus, my fate is in my hands, I make the final decision. My life is not predetermined. I choose whether I wish to know the mission of my life. I decide whether to do all in my power to accomplish it. Sometimes I complain that my destiny is too *hard*, but then I remember that God would have never given me a rock too heavy for me to carry. If he has chosen me for this mission, it means that I can carry it out. I just need to believe.

'Who am I? / A traveller resigned to walk far,' reads one of my early poems. And just like an interpreter, who translates between languages, I take the role of a storyteller to transform my life journey into a message that can be understood by others.

The Mandala of My Past, 2020
Acrylic and mixed media on circular canvas 50 cm
In private collection
Illustration by Alice Chudes

List of Illustrations
by Alice Chudes

All paintings illustrated here are originally in colour and can be found at www.store-alicechudes.com.

The Mandala of My Past, 2020
Acrylic and mixed media on circular canvas 50 cm
In private collection
    ** Refers to 'List of Illustrations' by Alice Chudes

The Pink-Golden Explosion of Love, 2020
Acrylic and mixed media on circular canvas 50 cm
    ** Refers to 'Acknowledgements'

The Purple Passion, 2020
Acrylic and mixed media on circular canvas 50 cm
    ** Refers to 'I Saw You in One Wicked and Forbidden Dream'

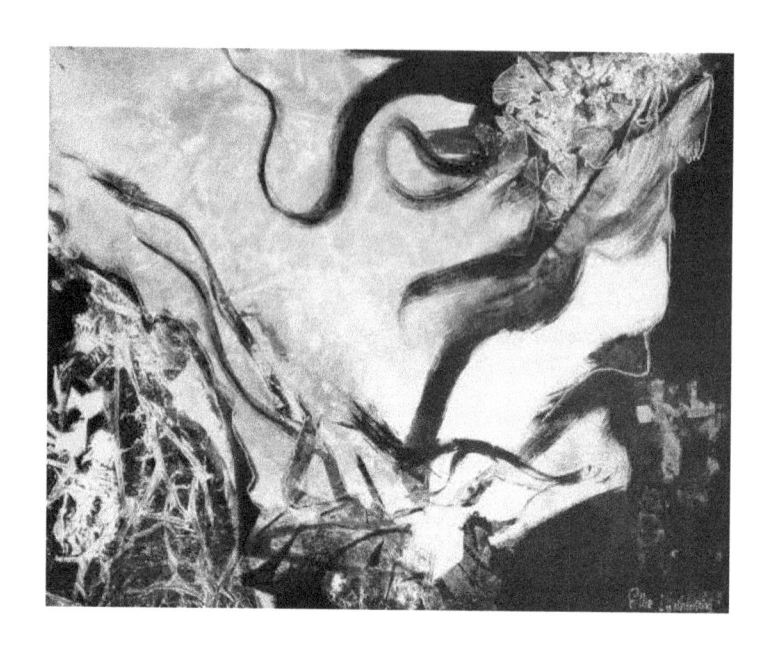

Feel and Liber, 2019
Mixed media on canvas 90 by 60 cm

    I am multidimensional. I have always taken risks. So, even if everything goes wrong, at least I feel alive pursuing it.
—Ellie Lasthiotaki

List of Illustrations
by Ellie Lasthiotaki

Most of the paintings illustrated here are originally in colour and can be found at www.ellielasthiotaki.com.

A Branch of Peace, 2019
Acrylic and resin on wood panel 35 by 15 cm
   ** *Refers to 'My Unicorn at the Genesis of the New World'*

A Chanting Phoenix, 2020
Acrylic on canvas 60 by 40 cm
   ** *Front page and frontispiece, refers to The Saga of a Chanting Phoenix collection of poetry*
   ** *Also refers to 'Walking in Your Footsteps'*

A Dancing Queen, 2015
Acrylic on canvas 90 by 60 cm
   ** *Refers to 'If I Were Your Queen!'*

A Girl with Roses, 2017
Acrylic on canvas 45 by 35 cm
   ** *Refers to 'You Are My Cup of Tea!'*

A Seed of Knowledge, 2020
Inspired by Alice Chudes' poem 'A Seed of Knowledge'
Acrylic and charcoal on paper 29 by 21 cm
   ** *Refers to 'A Seed of Knowledge'*

A Whole Half, 2016
Acrylic on paper 25 by 15 cm
In private collection
   ** *Refers to 'It Is Time to Act'*

Abyss, 2019
Acrylic and Chinese calligraphy ink on canvas 90 by 60 cm
    *** Refers to 'The Eye of the Perfect Storm'*

All It Takes Is a Flower, 2018
Acrylic on paper 20 by 15 cm
    *** Refers to 'A Thought of Gratitude'*

Beyond Senses, 2018
Acrylic, oil, inks, and pastels on canvas 90 by 60 cm
    *** Refers to 'A Medium in Love'*

Blossom Study, 2020
Mixed media on canvas 35 by 25 cm
    *** Refers to 'Knowledge Germinates the Enlightenment Seed'*

Blossoming Truth, 2019
Acrylic on canvas 25 by 25 cm
In private collection
    *** Refers to 'Truth Always Leaks Out'*

Carving Out My Path, 2019
Acrylic on paper 30 by 20 cm
    *** Refers to 'Destiny Is Carving Out My Path in Poetry'*

Cataclysm, 2015
Acrylic on canvas 90 by 60 cm
    *** Refers to 'The World on Fire'*

Circe, 2019
Acrylic on canvas 190 by 90 cm
In private collection
    *** Refers to 'Six Senses in Jerusalem'*

Colour the Paradise and Get In, 2018
Acrylic on canvas 90 by 60 cm
    *** Back page, Alice Chudes Portrait*
    *** Also refers to 'Love Is Way More Durable Than Hatred'*

Craving for You, 2019
Acrylic on wood panel 90 by 60 cm
   ** *Refers to 'Truth Is, You Never Left Me'*

Deep Kiss, 2020
Acrylic on canvas 90 by 60 cm
   ** *Refers to 'Metamorphosis: Painting the Mandala of My Past to Release My New Future'*

Detail, Seize the Day in Blues, 2020
Acrylic on wood panel 120 by 60 cm
In private collection
   ** *Refers to 'A Play on Words'*

Devoted Dreams, 2018
Acrylic on canvas 90 by 60 cm
In private collection
   ** *Refers to 'A Sight of the Parallel World'*

Dispersing Nyctophobia, 2020
Acrylic on paper 30 by 25 cm
   ** *Refers to 'Light Through a Kaleidoscope Heals in Time of Self-Doubt'*

Don't Cry, 2015
Acrylic on paper 30 by 25 cm
   ** *Refers to 'A Motherly Gaze'*

Dreamy Sunset, 2020
Acrylic on canvas 90 by 90 cm
   ** *Refers to 'Une Heureuse Pensée à Propos de la Vie' / 'A Happy Thought About Life'*

E-motions, 2019
Acrylic on canvas 90 by 90 cm
   ** *Refers to 'A Million Shattered Pieces'*

Echoes of Spring, 2015
Acrylic on canvas 90 by 60 cm
In private collection
   ** *Refers to 'Dancing Snow'*

Embracing the World, 2017
Acrylic on canvas 90 by 60 cm
   ** *Refers to 'Creator's Calling'*

Endoscopy, 2020
Acrylic on paper 30 by 20 cm
   ** *Refers to 'Revelations in Turbulent Times'*

Entanglement 1 and 2, 2019
From the series of 'Entanglement'
Acrylic and ink on canvas 120 by 60 cm
   ** *Refers to 'A Cry of My Soul'*

Entanglement 3, 2016
From the series of 'Entanglement'
Acrylic on canvas 90 by 60 cm
   ** *Refers to 'A Night Silver Lining'*

Feel and Liber, 2019
Mixed media on canvas 90 by 60 cm
   ** *Refers to 'A Restless Traveller'*
   ** *Also refers to 'List of Illustrations' by Ellie Lasthiotaki*

Fire and Ice, 2018
Acrylic on paper 35 by 25 cm
   ** *Refers to 'Une Vague Idée de l'Amour' / 'A Faint Image of Love'*

Floating, 2020
From the series of 'Life Has Many Turns'
Acrylic on wood panel 20 by 20 cm
   ** *Refers to 'Subject to Interpretation'*

Fractured Imperfections 1, 2018
From the series of 'Fractured Imperfections'
Acrylic and gold leaf on paper 15 by 15 cm
In private collection
    *** Refers to 'À l'Amie du Cœur' / 'To My Dear Friend'*

Fractured Imperfections 2, 2018
From the series of 'Fractured Imperfections'
Acrylic and gold leaf on canvas 90 by 60 cm
    *** Refers to 'A Leap of Faith'*

Fractured Imperfections 3, 2018
From the series of 'Fractured Imperfections'
Acrylic and gold leaf on paper 15 by 15 cm
In private collection
    *** Refers to 'My Anointed Future'*

Fractured Imperfections 4, 2018
From the series of 'Fractured Imperfections'
Acrylic and gold leaf on paper 15 by 15 cm
In private collection
    *** Refers to 'A Glimpse at Apocalypse'*

Fractured Imperfections 5, 2018
From the series of 'Fractured Imperfections'
Acrylic and gold leaf on paper 15 by 15 cm
In private collection
    *** Refers to 'A Message in a Bottle'*

Fractured Imperfections 6, 2018
From the series of 'Fractured Imperfections'
Acrylic and gold leaf on paper 15 by 15 cm
In private collection
    *** Refers to 'My Outside-the-Box Mantra'*

Fractured Imperfections 7, 2018
From the series of 'Fractured Imperfections'
Acrylic and gold leaf on paper 15 by 15 cm
    ** *Refers to 'Reunion: It Is Not Too Late!'*

Fractured Imperfections 8, 2018
From the series of 'Fractured Imperfections'
Acrylic and gold leaf on paper 15 by 15 cm
In private collection
    ** *Refers to 'Tu Es Mon Étoile Filante' / 'You Are My Shooting Star'*

Fractured Imperfections 9, 2018
From the series of 'Fractured Imperfections'
Acrylic and gold leaf on paper 15 by 15 cm
In private collection
    ** *Refers to 'La Brume de Demain' / 'The Mist of Destiny'*

Fractured Imperfections 10, 2018
From the series of 'Fractured Imperfections'
Acrylic and gold leaf on paper 15 by 15 cm
In private collection
    ** *Refers to 'Une Lettre d'Amour' / 'A Love Letter'*

Fractured Imperfections 11, 2018
From the series of 'Fractured Imperfections'
Acrylic and gold leaf on paper 15 by 15 cm
    ** *Refers to 'Catching My Muse, My Firebird'*

Fractured Imperfections 12, 2018
From the series of 'Fractured Imperfections'
Acrylic and gold leaf on paper 15 by 15 cm
In private collection
    ** *Refers to 'Mon Cœur Rayonne' / 'A Beam from My Heart'*

Freedom Is Bravery, 2017
Acrylic on canvas 150 by 100 cm
    ** *Refers to 'La Soif de Liberté' / 'Thirst for Freedom'*

Hidden Letters of Love, 2020
Acrylic and gold leaf on paper 35 by 25 cm
    *** Refers to 'A Fortune Stroke of Serendipity'*

Human Study 1, 2016
Acrylic on paper 20 by 15 cm
    *** Refers to 'Oh, Baby, Hear My Questions!'*

Human Study 2, 2016
Acrylic on paper 20 by 15 cm
    *** Refers to 'One Dreadful Step Ahead'*

I Am Enough, 2014
Acrylic and pastels on paper 20 by 15 cm
    *** Refers to 'A Hymn for My Subconscious Mind'*

I Own My Dreams, 2019
Acrylic on paper 30 by 20 cm
    *** Refers to 'Dreams Are Answers from the Subconscious'*

In Love with This View, 2020
Acrylic on canvas 90 by 60 cm
    *** Refers to 'Thanksgiving to God'*

Impulse, 2019
From the series of 'Fractured Imperfections'
Acrylic on canvas 92 by 92 cm
    *** Refers to 'Defining Timelessness'*

Liquid Gold Duality Defying Rocks, 2019
Acrylic and gold leaf on wood panel 25 by 25 cm
In private collection
    *** Refers to 'Sacrificial Lambs'*

Little Things Make Me Happy, 2019
Acrylic on paper 30 by 20 cm
    *** Refers to 'Happiness Is to Be in Tune with the World'*

My Echo of Desire, 2020
Acrylic on canvas 90 by 60 cm
    ** Refers to 'Abundance Is Being Wealthy with What Is Within One's Grasp'

My Little Ballerina, 2016
Acrylic on paper 40 by 30 cm
    ** Refers to 'Une Lettre à Ma Fille' / 'A Letter to My Daughter'

Meditating, 2017
Acrylic on canvas 90 by 60 cm
    ** Refers to 'Le Courant de la Vie' / 'The Current of Life'

Odysseas, 2019
Acrylic on canvas 30 by 20 cm
    ** Refers to 'Phoenix's Saga in Chanted Poetry'

Otherworldly Perception, 2019
Acrylic on canvas 100 by 100 cm
    ** Refers to 'My Musings About Life'

Pensive, 2017
Acrylic on canvas 90 by 60 cm
    ** Refers to '#MeToo'

Reminiscence of Fragrances, 2016
Watercolour on paper 40 by 30 cm
    ** Refers to 'Ink's Power to Heal'

Sea Is the Mirror of Ourselves, 2018
Acrylic and oil on canvas 150 by 100 cm
    ** Refers to 'Foreword by Vladimir Guevarra: Reading Alice Chudes' Romantic and Relatable Verses'

Self-Portrait, 2016
Acrylic on canvas 45 by 35 cm
    ** Refers to 'It Is Hard Dealing with a Poet' by Vladimir Guevarra

Self-Portrait, 2018
Acrylic on canvas 20 by 20 cm
    ** *Refers to 'A Weeping Soul in the River of Life'*

Soaring Spirit, 2020
Acrylic on wood panel 15 by 15 cm
    ** *Refers to 'Truth Is What You Hear When You Stand Still'*

Strangers, 2015
Acrylic on paper 20 by 15 cm
    ** *Refers to 'Two Acquainted Strangers'*

Take a Breath In, 2018
Acrylic on canvas 90 by 60 cm
    ** *Back page, Elle Lasthiotaki Self-Portrait*
    ** *Also refers to 'Tombée Amoureuse' / 'Fallen in Love'*

The Bridge of Hope, 2016
Acrylic on canvas 90 by 60 cm
    ** *Refers to 'The Music of My Heart'*

The Choice Is Yours, 2020
Inspired by Alice Chudes' poem 'Dove's Happiness Scent'
Acrylic and charcoal on paper 30 by 20 cm
    ** *Refers to 'Deux Colombes, l'Âme de l'Océan' / 'Dove's Happiness Scent'*

The Desire, 2018
From the series of 'Life Has Many Turns'
Acrylic on wood panel 100 by 100 cm
    ** *Refers to 'Enlevée par le Vent' / 'The Other Side of the Mirror'*

The Golden Paths, 2015
Acrylic and gold leaf on canvas 40 by 30 cm
    ** *Refers to 'A Rhetorical Question for Motherland'*

The Hidden Urban Marvel, 2019
Acrylic on canvas 90 by 90 cm
In private collection
    *** Refers to 'La Fève de la Galette des Rois' / 'Twelfth Night Cake's Charm'*

The Light from Within, 2018
From the series of 'Fractured Imperfections'
Acrylic and gold leaf on paper 15 by 15 cm
In private collection
    *** Refers to 'I Wander. I Wonder. I Speak to the Stars'*

The Linear Path, 2015
Acrylic on canvas 90 by 60 cm
In private collection
    *** Refers to 'Will the World Ever Change?'*

The Magic of the Universe, 2017
Acrylic on canvas 15 by 15 cm
    *** Refers to 'A Blessing in Disguise'*

The Nebula Queen, 2017
Acrylic on wood panel 30 by 20 cm
In private collection
    *** Refers to 'My Poetry Interpretation'*

The Need of Spiritual Guidance in Chaos, 2019
Acrylic and silk screen on canvas 50 by 50 cm
    *** Refers to 'Wisdom Is an All-Encompassing Heavenly Ode'*

The Perfection of Nothingness, 2019
Mixed media on canvas 90 by 60 cm
In private collection
    *** Refers to 'An Illusion of Separation'*

The Promise of the Unexpected Light, 2018
Finalist at The International Artist Grand Prize Competition 2019, Taiwan
Acrylic on canvas 90 by 60 cm
    *** Refers to 'La Lumière Divine' / 'The Divine Light'*

The Tree of Happiness, 2016
Acrylic on canvas 90 by 60 cm
    *** Refers to 'L'Aspiration d'une Petite Fille' / 'The Yearning of a Little Girl'*

Through Your Eyes I Could Dream the Sky, 2019
Acrylic on canvas 40 by 40 cm
    *** Refers to 'Un Rêve de Midi' / 'A Midday Dream'*

Togetherness, 2020
Acrylic on paper 25 by 15 cm
    *** Refers to 'Love Grows the Wings to Touch Infinity'*

Tornado, 2018
Acrylic on wood panel 50 by 50 cm
In private collection
    *** Refers to 'Lost Without Hope'*

Two Is Better Than One, 2019
Acrylic and silk screen on canvas 30 by 30 cm
    *** Refers to 'Adieu to He Who Does Not Exist'*

Unearthly, 2018
Acrylic on wood panel 15 by 15 cm
    *** Refers to 'Soul Is an Intangible Quintessence of Life'*

Unpredictability, 2019
Acrylic on wood panel 60 by 50 cm
    *** Refers to 'Life Is a Rose with Thorns'*

Untitled, 2019
Acrylic on wood panel 55 by 55 cm
    *** Refers to 'An Unanswered Invitation'*

Who Am I? 2019
Acrylic on paper 20 by 20 cm
    *** Refers to 'The Hidden Sense of Life'*

Wild Thoughts, 2018
Acrylic on canvas 60 by 45 cm
   ** *Refers to 'I Wish I Were Not Alone'*

Windy Thoughts, 2018
Acrylic on canvas 120 by 60 cm
In private collection
   ** *Refers to 'Time Is Spiral Like DNA'*

Wine Bottle Study, 2016
Watercolours on paper 25 by 20 cm
   ** *Refers to 'The Secret Love Potion'*

Lightning Source UK Ltd.
Milton Keynes UK
UKHW012030090621
385222UK00001B/11